Remembering God's Word

Remembering God's Word

How to Improve Your Recall the Natural Way

by

Ed Rehbein

Unless indicated otherwise, Scripture references are from The Holy Bible, New International Version.

Printed and Bound in the
United States of America

Library of Congress Catalog Card Number: 90-55859
International Standard Book Number: 0-89900-359-1

ACKNOWLEDGEMENTS

I sincerely appreciate the support of many who, directly or indirectly, contributed to this book. I have learned much from the many fine books published about memory. Jerry Lucas' *Remember the Word* has been particularly helpful, and I have drawn upon many of the ideas presented there.

I am grateful to my friends and fellow Christians at the Cherokee Hills Church of Christ in Oklahoma City, for their interest in my Bible study classes and for their generous words of encouragement. My thanks also for their finanicial support as well as the financial support I receive from the North Beckley Church of Christ in Beckley, West Virginia, where I now serve as a Full-time Minister.

I also wish to thank my family and especially my wife Phyllis for believing in this book and in me.

Of course nothing could have been accomplished without the blessings of God. Him I humbly thank for the love of His Son and the truth of His Word.

TABLE OF CONTENTS

Part I
Getting Started

Part II
Learning the Basics of Memory Improvement

Part III
Applying Your Memory Skills

PART I
GETTING STARTED

CHAPTER ONE

Your God-Given Powers of Memory

Have you ever noticed that remembering a person's face is far easier than remembering their name? Even if considerable time has passed since you last saw someone, you will generally be able to recall his or her face, but the name may elude your memory. This suggests that your visual memory is superior to your memory for words. Because this seems to be true for most people, it prompted some fascinating scientific research reported by Dr. Ralph Haber in Scientific American (Haber 1970).

Groups of volunteers were shown over 2,500 photographic slides at the rate of one every ten seconds. One hour after viewing the last slide, the subjects were shown pairs of slides. Each pair contained one slide that they had viewed earlier and one slide, similar in appearance, that they had never seen before. When asked to identify the slide that they had seen previously, the subjects chose correctly an amazing 85 to 95% of the time. This led Dr. Haber to a startling conclusion, "The capacity of the memory for pictures may be unlimited."

This astonishing experiment illustrates that the mind of man is indeed one of God's most miraculous creations. Though mankind is continually building larger and faster electronic computers, man-made computers have yet to match the mind of man in storage capacity, visual perception, or creative thinking. Unfortunately, the skills of the mind are not always recognized and used. This is particularly true about memory. Many people lack confidence in their ability to remember, and most do not fully use the power of their memory.

The purpose of this book is to unlock the powers of memory that God has created in you. The methods of memory training taught here are simple and easy to use because they are based on the mind's natural abilities and tendencies. This is important, because those who have struggled through endless repetitions of scriptures or other Bible material realize that the rote method is not a comfortable, natural, or particularly enjoyable way to commit information to memory. In this book, the optimum number of repetitions and time to review will be taught, thus making even review enjoyable rather than a burden. In fact, all memorization and memory training can be fun when the mind's natural powers are consciously applied.

The Power of Visual Memory

Let's briefly examine some of these natural powers of the mind and see how memory improvement techniques stem from them. For example, the volunteers in Dr. Haber's experiment apparently had no special memory training, but merely used a God-given talent that we all have, the ability to recall visual images. Aware of this ability, many memory experts frequently employ it. In this book you will learn to employ it by converting to visual images the concepts, words, and even numbers that you encounter in Bible reading and study. Making these conversions is not difficult, and it will enable you to use the mind's powerful visual memory to store and recall anything concerning God's Word that is important to you.

Given an increased ability to remember, is there a possibility that you will simply run out of places to store memories? Again we must marvel at what God has created in us, for according to author Roy Gallant (1980, 66), "the human brain's capacity to store information is 10,000 times greater than that of the big computers today." Gallant further reports that our storage capacity is so vast that were we to continuously enter information into our brain at the maximum allowable rate from the time we are born to age 65, less than 10% of our storage capacity would be used. Perhaps this is why it is said that we only use 10% of our mind's capacity. Regardless, you certainly have the power to store in your mind as much of God's Word as you desire.

Association: The Natural Filing System of the Mind

The mind has other natural abilities that you will learn to develop in the chapters that follow. For instance, each new piece of information that you encounter is entered into your brain by connecting it to something that is already in the memory. The mind instinctively and automatically makes this connection. This process is called association.

Association is the mind's natural filing system. One way of illustrating this ability is through word associations. What is the first word that occurs to you when I say the word, "Cross"? Words that occur to a Christian might be "Jesus," "Savior," "Calvary," "crucifixion," "sacrifice," etc. The point is that in thinking of one thing, "Cross," another thought automatically follows. It follows because in the mind the two thoughts are linked or associated. Most thoughts are unconsciously associated and are oftentimes weakly linked. You will learn how to purposely and consciously make strong associations that will ensure easy recall at a future time.

Interest Stimulates Memory

Do we generally remember that which is boring, repetitious, dull, typical or unexciting? No, God seems to have created in us a mind that favors and remembers the unusual, the humorous, the interesting, the exciting, or the emotional. It is truly a great blessing that our minds are naturally attracted to the charms and variety of life that God has created for all to enjoy. This natural inclination of the mind can strengthen the recall of any subject matter, including God's Word. This is achieved by making associations humorous, colorful, action-packed, interesting, or unusual. These vivid associations will be naturally and easily recalled whenever you wish.

Actually this technique applies a broader concept in memory training. Creating vivid associations makes them interesting to the mind. This interest is vitally important in memory, for you remember what interests you. A classic example of the value of interest is that of a schoolboy who does poorly at remembering his multiplication facts, yet easily recalls the batting averages of numerous baseball players. He does not have a faulty memory, merely a different interest than his teacher. I am sure that you have family members or friends with an incredible memory for certain topics, topics that really interest them.

Interest enhances memory because interest creates concentration or focus, and focus enables information to be entered into the mind with fewer interfering thoughts. If the mind did not have the ability to tune out interference, it would soon become cluttered.

For example, while reading this book, you receive input from all your senses. Imagine trying to remember what was read if, with equal emphasis, you recalled the sound of the children playing in the next room, the smell of dinner being prepared, the feel of the chair beneath you, or the taste of the coffee that you drank. Fortunately our Creator designed our minds to be selective; you choose your focus or emphasis, and it is interest that establishes that focus. Because you are reading this book, you already have an interest in recalling God's Word and knowing it more deeply. Your interest in God's Word will be a great asset in memory training.

Patterns Simplify Memorization

Another fascinating quality of our mind is useful in

memory. Let me illustrate this quality with an example. If I list a series of ten numbers for you to memorize such as:

9 2 8 7 0 1 5 4 6 3.

it might prove very difficult. Scientific studies have shown that most people can hold, for a short time, about six or seven digits in their memory. A telephone number is about this size. With ten numbers most people need to study and repeat them several times to commit the sequence to memory.

Now I'll use the same ten digits but in a different order:

1 3 5 7 9 0 2 4 6 8.

Compare sequences and determine which is easier to memorize. Is the second sequence easier? Yes, because a pattern exists; first odd numbers from 1 to 9 are listed in ascending order followed by even numbers in ascending order. Did you notice this? You probably did, for our minds naturally look for patterns, order, or structure in the world around us. Essentially the second ten digit sequence was recognized by the mind as just two sequences, one of odd numbers and the other of even numbers. Instead of remembering ten bits of data, which is difficult, the mind naturally reduces it to two bits of data, which are easily memorized. Thus the mind consolidates large amounts of information into smaller chunks. This automatically facilitates data storage and recall.

Applying this skill in God's Word you will learn to organize and structure Bible knowledge so that it can be easily memorized. In fact, seeking structure or order to Bible information will improve not only your memory of the material but your understand ing of it as well. For as you seek the structure of new materi al, you will naturally gain a deeper understanding of its mean ing, logic, and purpose.

Learning to Develop Your Memory Skills

By now I hope you believe as I do that your memory is better than you think. All that is needed is a better understanding of how to fully develop the power of your memory. That is the purpose of this book.

Reviewed briefly in this chapter, the basic principles underlying memory improvement techniques will be detailed in Part II. The principles will be presented in a practical manner emphasizing specific tips and examples to assist your memory development. Armed with a knowledge of the basics, we will discuss in Part III how to apply your knowledge to remember God's Word in a variety of different settings. You will learn how to remember Bible sermons and classes, improve your recall of Bible reading, and memorize verses, chapters and even books of the Bible. You will be able to tailor your memory work to suit your individual needs and way of thinking.

Rather than present a rigid set of memory rules, this book will enable you to understand how memory works and will equip you with sufficient skills to accomplish your goals in remembering God's Word.

Truly God has blessed you with a mind that is naturally well equipped to study and remember His Word. He has not hidden Himself from you; rather He has revealed His nature through His Word and then given you the mental power to understand His Word. Indeed, the mind of man is such a marvel that it clearly points to a Creator even more marvelous.

CHAPTER TWO

The Blessings of Good Bible Recall

You are driving out of the parking lot after a pleasant morning at church, when someone asks you about the sermon you just heard. Your mind goes blank. Aside from the title and perhaps a few sketchy details, little is recalled. You stop for a moment and realize that the same is true for the Bible class you attended that morning. In introspection you sadly admit that in a few days perhaps all will be forgotten. The next day, while chatting with a friend, questions come up about the Bible. You search your memory for the answers, but grope for ideas in frustration. "Why can't I remember more about the Bible?" you ask. "Considering the time I've spent with God's Word, I should be further along in knowledge."

I am sure that this has happened to many of us at one

time or another, for most of the people that I know are not completely satisfied with their ability to remember things. Concerning the Word of God, it is even more disappointing when we fail to recall it as we should; yet, this does not have to be so. As we learned in chapter 1, God created in each of us a powerful memory; it needs merely to be harnessed through proper training.

But is it worth the effort to improve your memory? Absolutely, the blessings of good Bible recall are manifold. For example, without memory there is no learning, no accumulation of knowledge. If we are to mature as Christians as we are commanded, then surely we must grow in wisdom and knowledge of the Scriptures (Hebrews 5:12-6:1).

Resist Temptation

Besides satisfying the command to grow, good Bible recall will help us follow the example set for us by our Lord. When challenged by unrighteousness, Christ often quoted scripture as a defense. Christ's temptation by Satan is a good example. Though weak from 40 days of fasting, Christ did not yield, but with each temptation He answered first, "It is written" (Matthew 4:1-11). Christ defended Himself with the word of God, which He quoted from memory. He didn't hesitate or stop to search the Scriptures; He recalled them immediately.

Wouldn't it be wonderful if we, too, could call upon God's Word anywhere, at any time, simply by drawing upon our memory. It would be a powerful force, strengthening us spiritually and helping us to resist temptation. We will never equal our Lord's mastery of the Scriptures; however, He told us that it is sufficient just to be like Him (Matthew 10:24-25). Through good Bible recall, it is surely possible to approach this goal.

Meditate on His Word

Deuteronomy 6:4-9 taught the Jews to put God's Word on their hearts and as signs on their foreheads and hands. The Word of God was to be on their minds when they were sitting, walking, even when lying down or rising up. At all times they were to be ready to teach their children the commandments of God. In a beautiful way, it was meant to inspire the Jews to intimately know and dwell on God's Word.

Unfortunately, they interpreted the commandment literally and began wearing phylacteries (Matthew 23:5). Phylacteries were strips of parchment with scriptures inscribed on them. They bound the phylacteries to their foreheads and hands to fulfill the commands of Deuteronomy 6:8.

The Jews missed the intent of God's wishes, but we need not. Today, with good Bible recall we will please God by inscribing His commands not on our foreheads, but in our minds. Further more, by recalling God's Word from memory at any time, we can easily meditate on His Word while sitting, standing, lying down, or even while driving. In fact I have enjoyed many pleasant hours behind the wheel recalling from memory chapters of the Bible. Just imagine! That commute to work would be fun if God's Word was played over and over in your mind. Though it sounds a bit far-fetched, it is possible through memory improvement systems.

Teach More Effectively

Christ also implored His disciples to teach others about Him (Mark 16:15-16). Moreover, in the New Testament we are encouraged to be prepared "in season and out of season" to teach and preach the gospel to anyone who should ask (2 Timothy 4:2, 1 Peter 3:15). These scriptures do not require that all of us become prominent gospel evangelists, but they should inspire us to know our Bibles better. How many times are we frustrated or disappointed by failing to recall the right scriptures just when they are needed most? Wouldn't it be wonderful to have God's Word so firmly planted in the mind that the right Bible-based solutions are available when they are really desired? This, too, is within our grasp through Bible memory training.

Fathom the Mind of God

Finally, because the results of Bible recall are cumulative, systematic study habits and a trained memory will enable you to know the Bible as never before. Let me use an example from childhood to illustrate how Bible knowledge accumulates. When building a snowman, a child generally starts with a small snow ball, which is rolled along the ground. At first very little snow sticks to it, and the ball of snow grows slowly. As it gains size, though, much more snow sticks to it, and it swells in volume. Soon it becomes too big to push.

In a way, our mind gathers knowledge similarly. When little is known about God's Word, it is difficult to learn more about it. Nevertheless, as Bible knowledge increases, new information is progressively easier to assimilate. Memory training then pays great dividends by promoting the accumulation of an ever-growing wealth of Bible knowledge. This eventually produces a comprehensive view of the Bible in which the unity and harmony of God's Word becomes increasingly evident.

This is truly a great blessing, for it is through God's Word that we best know Him. True, the marvels of His Creation yield a glimpse of God's majesty; yet it is in His Word that God most clearly reveals His mind to us. To know and recall God's Word, then, is to fathom more perfectly the nature of God.

Many are the blessings of good Bible recall. It will help us to resist temptation, to meditate on His Word, to teach more effectively, and to understand the mind of God. It will enrich our Christian lives and strengthen our discipleship, for as Christ spoke in John 8:31-32:

"If you abide in My word, then you are truly disciples of Mine; and you shall know the truth, and the truth shall make you free."

CHAPTER THREE

An Example of How to Remember God's Word

Before considering the basics of memory improvement covered in Part II, let me give an example of an easy way to remember some information about the Bible. By drawing on your powers of visualization and association, this example illustrates how the mind's natural abilities and tendencies are employed in memory techniques. To heighten interest, I will add a little touch of the unusual or humorous. Let's begin by memorizing, in correct order, the 12 books of the Minor Prophets: Hosea, Joel, Amos, Obadiah, Jonah, Micah, Nahum, Habakkuk, Zephaniah, Haggai, Zechariah, and Malachi. In my experience, few people already know the order of these books, so the example should demonstrate the effectiveness of the memory techniques. As I describe some word pictures to you, try to visualize them in your mind's eye as vividly as you can. Just relax and enjoy the exercise.

Memorizing the First Six Minor Prophets

Start by picturing a big brown fire hose. The "hose" will remind you of Hosea. Gobs of red jello are pouring out of the hose. The "jello" should remind you of the prophet Joel. The red jello is squirting all over a man, and he is becoming "a mess." "A mess" stands for Amos. Amos resents being covered with jello and in his anger falls onto an "old bed and dies" (Obadiah). The bed rises up, and a whale swims out from underneath it. The whale is a reminder about the story of Jonah. The whale opens his mouth and out drives "my car" (Micah).

That is the first six books of the Minor Prophets. Review the preceding paragraph right now, and then close your eyes and try to visualize the entire sequence of pictures. The names of the Minor Prophets are being transformed into pictures because your visual memory is superior to your memory for words. The pictures of the prophets are created using associations, in most cases letting similarity of sound link the name to the picture, such as Joel and "jello," and Amos and "a mess." Finally to generate interest, the pictures are vivid and humorous; this inscribes them firmly in your memory.

Memorizing the Last Six Minor Prophets

Now for the last six Minor Prophets. "My car" (Micah)

rams into a man's knee and "knees him" (Nahum). The man hunches over in pain as if he "has a back ache." "Has a back ache" should remind you of Habukkuk. His backache causes him to cry, and to stop crying he "zips an eye" shut. "Zip an eye" stands for Zephaniah. The tears roll down onto his beard, which is scruffy and makes him appear "haggard" (Haggai). The man totes a white "sack of rye" (Zechariah) over his shoulder. He sets the sack of rye down, pulls a cow out of it, and shoves the cow into a mailbox. He "mails a cow" to remind you of Malachi. Now review all the images and associations to the names. Then try to recall, in order, the 12 Minor Prophets. Table 3-1 summarizes the memory scheme to help you review.

This is one example of several methods that will enable Bible knowledge to be remembered using the natural, God-given abilities of your mind. Do methods such as this one really work? Yes, indeed! While teaching a class on the Minor Prophets, I used this very scheme to help the class remember the order of the books. I also included other word pictures to add detail about the content of each book.

My Minor Prophets class surveyed one book each week and finished the study in about three months. At the end of three months, we devoted a class period to review. To really test our recall of the Minor Prophets, we closed our Bibles, put aside our notes, and discussed each book entirely from memory. Even though considerable time had elapsed since our first class, everyone recalled the mental pictures and their meaning relative to the Minor Prophets. In addition, the material that we memorized prompted us to recall other facts and principles applicable to the Minor

Prophets. As we shall see in later chapters, just retaining a few bits of information firmly in the memory assists the recall of much more information that was not specifically memorized.

The students and I left the review class in a buoyant mood. As a teacher I felt satisfied knowing that I had imparted God's Word in such a way that it could not be easily forgotten. The students were happy, too, for they had gained confidence in their ability to memorize and were pleased that the hours of Bible study were well spent. The lesson we all shared was that learning and remembering God's Word does not have to be a chore; rather it may be an enjoyable and rewarding experience. After reading this book, I hope that you will feel this way, too.

Table 3-1 The Minor Prophets

	The Mental Picture	**The Prophet**
1.	A brown fire *hose* is	Hosea
2.	Squirting red *jello*	Joel
3.	On a man, making him *a mess*	Amos
4.	He falls on an *old bed and dies*	Obadiah
5.	A *whale* swims out from under the bed	Jonah
6.	And opens his mouth. *My car* drives out	Micah
7.	The car *knees him*	Nahum
8.	He hunches over in pain as if he *has a backache*	Habakkuk
9.	He cries and *zips an eye* shut to stop it	Zephaniah
10.	A tear falls on his beard, which is *haggard*	Haggai
11.	He totes a big white *sack of rye*	Zechariah
12.	He pulls a cow out of the sack and *mails a cow*	Malachi

PART II
LEARNING THE BASICS OF MEMORY IMPROVEMENT

CHAPTER FOUR

Association, Visualization, and Chaining: A Powerful Combination

Chapter 1 introduced you to some natural skills of the mind that relate to memory. In this chapter you will learn how to combine some of these skills when you wish to memorize Bible material. Specifically, you will learn how to combine the processes of association, visualization, and chaining. When melded together, these three processes are a powerful team, one which will help you to convert information from the Bible into a form that your mind can easily store and recall. You will learn other techniques in this book for memorizing material; however, understanding this combination of techniques will get you off to a good start toward "Remembering God's Word." Let's begin by examining in more detail the process of association.

Association

Did you ever wonder how the mind absorbs new information? How does it learn, and where does it file new data in the memory? According to memory expert, Dr. Bruno Furst, "We learn and remember everything that is new to us only by connecting it with something that we already know" (Furst 1972, 31). These connections, called associations, are vital to developing a good memory. Just as a library uses a card catalog to file the location of all its books, the mind uses associations to file information. The major difference between the mind and a library is that the mind's system is far superior because through association many more cross-references are constructed.

As a new piece of information enters the mind, it is associated with something already stored in the memory. For example, in the previous chapter you learned a system for recalling the 12 Minor Prophets. To remember Hosea, the new piece of data, you associated it with something already familiar to your mind, a brown fire hose. Once the two ideas are connected or associated in the mind, thinking of one will automatically stimulate the recall of the other. Thus when you visualize a brown fire hose in the memory scheme, the prophet Hosea springs to mind. It happens quite automatically because that is how the mind naturally works, by association. One thought, in this case a hose, serves to cue another thought, namely Hosea.

The mind makes associations all the time; in fact, most of the time you are not even aware of the process. Often, though, this leads to weak associations, and because weak associations are difficult to recall, your remembrance is hindered. One secret to a sharp memory is to consciously form strong associations. Learning to actively create strong associations will multiply the accuracy and capacity of your memory. In order to learn how to build these strong associations, let's examine the types of associations that the mind makes.

Types of Associations

The importance of associations in the thought process was first recognized by Greek and Roman philosophers. Aristotle studied associations and classified them, and today the types of associations are well understood.

Perhaps the most frequent type of association is similarity. In this instance, two items are associated in the mind because of something they have in common. The similarity may be of sound, such as hose and Hosea. This is a particularly useful type of association, one which I employ frequently in Bible memorization. Other associations can be based on a similarity of meaning, such as synonyms.

Just as similar things are easily associated, so are opposites or contrasting items. Examples are black and white, love and hate, and night and day. If you are a logical thinker, you might build a lot of cause and effect associations, such as linking thunder with lightening and matches with fire.

Another common type of association is that of matching pairs, as in salt and pepper. Matching pairs from the Bible could be Noah and the ark or Jonah and the whale, because each member of these pairs is usually thought of in connection with the other member.

Whole and part is another way to associate thoughts. I often employ whole and part association in Bible memorization. For example, I associate a reference to God speaking (a part) to the Bible (the whole).

Associations can be further classified and sub-divided, but do not be alarmed; understanding the theory of associations is not essential to creating associations. Your mind automatically creates associations. God made it that way; in fact, it would be very difficult for you not to make associations. Memory training merely attempts to assist and strengthen that natural process.

I have listed the major types of associations so that you might experiment with them to determine which work best with your way of thinking. Some people like to use rhyming associations, which are similarities of sound, while others prefer more structured associations, such as whole and part or cause and effect. I find associations using similarity of sound and matching pairs to be most compatible with the way I think and frequently use them in constructing associations.

Using Associations to Memorize

Now that you know a little more about associations, let's use them to memorize a scripture. Afterwards we will analyze the process so that you can learn how to form your own associations. This exercise will also acquaint you with the use of visualization and chaining.

Although this popular verse may be familiar to you already, let's memorize the first Beatitude, "Blessed are the poor in spirit, for theirs is the kingdom of heaven"

(Matt. 5:3). We will study scripture memorizing in more detail in chapter 12, but for now let's just examine a few of the basic principles in memorizing.

To memorize this scripture word-for-word, we begin by selecting the key elements of the sentence, which are usually the nouns, verbs, and important descriptors. For Matthew 5:3 these are "blessed," "poor," "spirit," "kingdom," and "heaven." Just memorizing these words in the correct order is all the help your mind needs to recall the entire scripture verbatim. These key sentence components serve as cues to help your mind fill in all of the other words in the sentence. It generally happens quite automatically, and further demonstrates just how remarkable the mind is.

To memorize these words let's form some associations. Spirit could be associated with a ghost, a similarity of meaning. The spirit is poor, so the ghost will have empty pockets. In the context of this scripture, "blessed are" means "happy are"; therefore, let's make the ghost happy. Now we can represent the beginning of the first Beatitude as a happy ghost pulling his pockets inside out to show that he is poor. This mental picture symbolizes "Blessed are the poor in spirit."

The remainder of the verse can also be converted into symbols by associations. For example, kingdom, the whole, can be represented as a crown, a part. Likewise, heaven could be associated with a cloud.

Thus, to remember the first Beatitude simply picture in your mind's eye a happy ghost with empty pockets reaching up to possess a cloud with a crown on it. Seems a little silly doesn't it. Nevertheless because of the way God fashioned your mind, it can easily recall this mental picture, and more importantly, it can then translate the picture back to Matthew 5:3, word-for-word. Think of the mental picture right now, and see if the words of Matthew 5:3 are recalled.

Perhaps you are thinking that you could just as easily repeat the verse 10 times or so and know it equally well. This might be true, but to remember more scriptures or longer scriptures, the association and visualization method works faster and lasts longer. For example, using this method in chapter 12 you will learn how to memorize, verbatim, scriptures that contain over 50 words.

During one Bible class that I taught, we used association, visualization, and chaining to memorize all of the Beatitudes, word-for-word, and the rest of the Sermon on the Mount, topic-by topic. At the end of the study, everyone in the class could recall the material quite accurately.

Convert Abstract Items into Concrete Ones

Now that you have memorized Matthew 5:3, let's analyze how this was accomplished using association, visualization, and chaining. By associations, the first step was to translate all abstract concepts into concrete terms. This aided recall because the mind grasps and relates to concrete subjects much more readily than to abstract ones. Jesus, the Master Teacher, knew this well and employed this technique frequently in His teaching.

A good example is the way in which Jesus explained to His followers the kingdom of heaven, which is a rather abstract, spiritual concept. He taught them in parables, His earthly stories with a heavenly meaning. Christ did this to illustrate the attributes of the kingdom of heaven in terms that would be easy to understand. Knowing perfectly the mind of man, Jesus often translated abstract ideas into concrete ones in order to make the Word of God understandable and memorable to all men.

Thus we should not be surprised that by following Jesus' example, we will learn and recall more of God's Word. For instance, to memorize the first Beatitude we translated several abstractions into the concrete. The kingdom of heaven became a cloud with a crown, the poor in spirit became a ghost with empty pockets. Not only are these concrete objects easier for the mind to grasp, they are also more readily visualized than their abstract counterparts.

Paint Vivid Mental Pictures

This is critical in memory improvement, for most Bible knowledge that you may wish to remember will be best stored in your mind as images or pictures. As discussed in chapter 1, the experiment by Haber (1970) illustrates the power of your visual memory, which is nearly unlimited. Hence, a key ingredient in good recall of any material is to have a visual impression, a mental picture of it. Once this is achieved, the mental image will remain intact within your memory for a considerable time. Therefore, the second step in this memorization technique is to visualize the material that you are studying. Do this by creating mental pictures out of the concrete items that you have created by association.

To take advantage of another property of the mind, its

inclination for the unusual and interesting, it is best to create your mental pictures as vividly as possible. These vivid images are inscribed more deeply in your mind than lifeless ones and are, therefore, more easily recalled. Painting vivid images in your mind is fun and generally turns memory work into a joy rather than a burden. So simply relax and allow your imagination to run free.

Here are some tips to help you create vivid pictures in your mind's eye. Action is a key ingredient for your pictures. Make them come alive and move, animate them. Do you remember the Minor Prophets memory aid? It was loaded with action connecting one symbol to another. Jello was squirting all over; a car drove out of a whale's mouth; a cow was pushed into a mailbox. It was a pretty busy picture. As you begin to construct your mental pictures, be sure to include action.

The scenes described above contained humor as well as action. I cannot keep from chuckling a little when I imagine that red jello squirting all over "Amos." Because humor injects interest into the image, be sure to include plenty of laughs in your mental picture.

Painting your pictures in technicolor also adds interest. Color adds an extra dimension of richness and texture to your image that is not easily forgotten.

Emotions animate your pictures, too, so include them. If you are able to include yourself and your emotions into the pictures, that is even better. Also try exaggerating the size or shape of objects. An odd or unusual perspective always seems to captivate our attention and impress an image on the mind. Again referring to our Minor Prophets example, we pulled a cow out of a sack of rye and pushed it into a mail box! That definitely required some alterations of size.

That scene also illustrates another technique for making your pictures memorable; put things out-of-place. This generally jars the imagination and firms the image in the memory. The whale swimming out from under the bed is also a good example to illustrate this concept.

If you use these techniques, your mental visualizations may seem somewhat silly, even childlike, to you. If they do, great! You have succeeded in creating images that will be remembered long after cold, lifeless, and logical ones are forgotten. Children are noted for their keen memories. They are also noted for active imaginations, a powerful interest in the world about them, and an inclination to fantasize. I suspect that their good memories stem at least in part from these qualities. So relax, let your imagination go, and create interesting pictures. They will enable you to remember God's Word to a degree that will astound you.

Chaining

The third and final step in this memorization technique is called "chaining." Just as a chain is built by connecting links, images can be linked or chained together in your mind. For example, the names of the 12 Minor Prophets were linked together one-by-one in your mind using the memory scheme presented in chapter 3. The images created for Matthew 5:3 were similarly linked.

As long as the information is linked together in the correct order in your memory by chaining, accurately recalling the material is easy. Just start by thinking of the first image or link. The thought of the first image will, by association, automatically stimulate the thought of the second image, which in turn stimulates the recall of the third image and so on. This recall process will continue until all the images are remembered in the correct order. It is just like reeling in a chain one link at a time.

This is the way your mind naturally files and retrieves information, and capitalizing on this ability makes recall easy. In fact, nearly an unlimited number of items can be chained together in your memory.

Your mind can truly store and recall an amazing volume of material through association, visualization, and chaining. These mental powers were granted to you by our Almighty Creator, and if they are fully appreciated and used, they can help fill your mind with the Word of God.

Indeed we possess such great potential that we should glorify God as David did in Psalm 139:14, "I praise you because I am fearfully and wonderfully made."

CHAPTER FIVE

Numbers: Turn Them Into Pictures

Which do you think would be easier to remember: the number 928,427,109,750 or a bonfire of neckties and pickles? The bonfire picture is usually much easier for most people to recall. Now for the surprise! Numbers can be converted into pictures. Using a special system called the "number code," 928,427,109,750 can be transformed into that crazy bonfire. The number code converts numbers into consonant sounds, and after mastering the code for numbers 0-9, you will be able to transform any number into a picture. You will even understand how a bonfire of neckties and pickles can help you recall perfectly that imposing string of numbers, 928,427,109,750. Numbers generally present a problem in memory, primarily because they are intangible, mathematical concepts and

and are not as easily grasped as tangible items. Numbers may also overload the memory merely by the shear volume of them, such as the numbers in the preceding paragraph. Nevertheless, numbers are very important to some kinds of Bible memory work, especially scripture locations. Memorizing a scripture is fun and satisfying, but it is also important to recall its place in the Bible. Although you memorized the first Beatitude in chapter 4, you now need the ability to file its location, Matthew 5:3, in your memory as well.

Knowing the number code system will expand your memory in another significant way, too. Picture a group of post office boxes, all with a number on the door. Behind each door is a piece of information that you wish to recall, and you do so merely by remembering the box number. As you think of the box number, the information within the box immediately appears in your mind. This seemingly magical process is called the "peg system," and it will help you remember everything from your grocery list, to the books of the Bible, to the sermon that you heard last Sunday. I believe that you will enjoy knowing how to use it.

The Number Code

But first, let's learn the number code system. This system was developed over many centuries, and by the 19th Century assumed its present form (Furst 1972, 110). Pick up any memory book today and you will find this practical and useful system.

The number code translates numbers into letters, or

more specifically into the sounds of letters. It is a phonetically based system in which each number from 0 to 9 is assigned a sound made by a consonant. Table 5-1 explains how the numbers 0-9 are coded into letters.

As you can see by Table 5-1, the number code is designed to be easily remembered. Visual cues or associations tie the number to its assigned letter. The number of downstrokes required to write a "t," "n," or "m" tells you which numbers these letters represent. The letters representing "6," "7," "8," and "9" resemble the shape of the numbers in some way or another. The code for zero and four is related to how these numbers are spelled. Shaping your left hand into an "L" reminds you of the code for five.

Table 5-1 The Number Code

Code	How To Recall
1 = t	"t" has one downstroke
2 = n	"n" is written with two downstrokes
3 = m	"m" is written with three downstrokes
4 = r	"r" is the last letter in "four"
5 = l	"L" is 50 in Roman numerals. You can also form an "L" with your left hand using five fingers
6 = j	A capital "J" reversed resembles a 6
7 = k	Lean two 7's together like this and you have a capital "K"
8 = f	A script "f" has two loops that look like an 8
9 = p	A backwards "P" resembles a 9
0 = z	The first letter in zero is "z"

Now that each digit from 0-9 has an assigned letter, numbers can be represented by words. To form words, though, you will need vowels. To make it easy to build words by adding vowels, all vowels are neutral, that is, they have no assigned number. In addition, the letters "w" and "y" are treated as vowels and have no assigned number. Let me illustrate how this works with some examples.

For instance, the Old Testament is comprised of thirty-nine books. Translating 39 into a word by the number code might be done as follows: 3=m and 9=p, so insert an "o" between them and you have "mop." If you can picture in your mind a mop on every page of your Old Testament you will probably not forget that it contains 39 books.

How would you memorize the location of Matthew 5:3, the verse we studied in the preceding chapter? One approach to recalling the chapter and verse reference, Mt. 5:3, would be to convert 5:3 into "lime" (l=5, i is a vowel with no value, m=3, and e is also a vowel with no value). Put the happy ghost with empty pockets on a juicy green "lime," and you will probably recall that "Blessed are the poor in spirit" is found at chapter 5, verse 3.

To make it easier to spell words from the number code, other consonants have been assigned to the numbers according to the sound the consonants make. Table 5-2 explains the additions to the number code.

Table 5-2 Additional Consonants

1 "d" sounds like "t" and is also made with one downstroke

6 The sound of a "j" is close to that of a soft "g" as in gentle, "ch" as in chew, and "sh" as in shoe.

7 The hard "g" sound as in gag or the hard "c" sound as in cat are similar to the sound of a "k."

8 Since "f" and "v" sound similar, both may be used for 8

9 Because "p" and "b" sound similar, both are used for 9

0 "s" and a soft "c" as in city sound like a "z" and are substituted for 0.

Now the number code is complete. Combining Tables 5-1 and 5-2, the number code looks like this:

1 = t,d	6 = j, g (soft), ch, sh
2 = n	7 = k, g (hard), c (hard)
3 = m	8 = f, v
4 = r	9 = p, b
5 = l	0 = z, s, c (soft)

Will this number code really help you recall numbers? Yes, indeed! After mastering the code, you can convert any number into a word. If you convert the number into a word that is easily pictured by your mind's eye, you have a quick and accurate way to recall that number. Do you remember that number quoted at the beginning of this chapter? Perhaps not, but you may vaguely recall a bonfire of neckties and pickles. Let's apply the number code to translate that bonfire picture back into numbers:

a ***bonfire*** of ***neckties*** and ***pickles***
9 28 4   2 7 1 0   9 75 0

That is the number from the beginning of the chapter. With the number code that 12 digit number was reduced to a simple mental picture, a picture that will seem effortless to recall compared to the number itself. In fact, using the code any number can be transformed into a word or a group of words, thereby making it much easier to remember.

The Peg System

The number code serves you in another way, too; with it you can implement the "peg system." The peg system is an interesting and quite useful method for storing information. The system establishes in your mind numbered locations or "pegs" where any type of data can be stored.

I like to think of the locations as numbered post office boxes in which you may toss anything that you wish to remember. The information remains in the box until you mentally go to it by thinking of the box number. When you think of that number, the information that you stored there will appear in your mind. It is truly a powerful system for improving your memory.

I frequently employ the peg system when listening to a sermon. Generally the speaker numbers the main topics of the lesson or at least divides it into discreet points. As I listen, I store each point on mentally numbered pegs, usually just pegs #1, #2, #3 and so on. After the sermon, I merely think of each peg number, and the points of the lesson are immediately recalled. I will teach you how to do this in chapter 9, but for now let's learn how to operate the peg system.

Using the number code, ten standard pictures or pegs are established to represent the numbers 1-10. Here are the pictures that I use:

1 = tea (cup)	6 = jaw (bone)
2 = Noah	7 = key
3 = Ma	8 = ivy
4 = rye (bread)	9 = bee
5 = law	10 = toes

Now to use the peg system, merely create a mental picture of point #1, and put a tea cup in that picture. For item #2, again form a picture of it, and this time put Noah in it. For the remaining items, just follow the same procedure. When you wish to recall the information in peg #1, simply visualize a tea cup and the picture created with that tea cup will come to mind. To help you better understand the procedure, let's memorize the Ten Commandments using the peg system.

Memorizing the Ten Commandments

The first commandment is "You shall have no other gods before me" (Exod. 20:3). The peg for #1 is a tea cup; so visualize a throne (a symbol for God) within a giant tea cup. The throne is sweeping away idols from in front of it. When you recall this image it should remind you that God wants no other gods before Him. The second commandment is "You shall not make for yourself an idol . . . or worship them" (Exod. 20:4-5). Peg #2 is Noah; this time imagine Noah standing in front of an idol and lifting up people who are bowing down to it. Noah is keeping the people from worshipping an idol.

The third commandment reads "You shall not misuse the name of the Lord your God" (Exod. 20:7). Because peg #3 is Ma, let's picture Ma washing out the mouth of a naughty little boy with soap. That traditional punishment for cursing should remind you that the third commandment is not to take the Lord's name in vain.

Commandment four is "Remember the Sabbath by keeping it holy" (Exod. 20:8). A piece of rye bread is peg #4; therefore, mentally picture a piece of rye bread poking holes (holy) in a bathtub. The bathtub has a sad face on it, which of course makes it a sad bath (Sabbath).

The fifth commandment is "Honor your Father and Mother" (Exod. 20:12). Peg #5 is law for which I use a lawman or policeman; so form a picture in your mind of a policeman in a blue suit. He places a crown on the heads of your mother and father to honor them.

Those are the first five commandments. Review them before proceeding with the remaining five, and then test your recollection. For instance, think of the third peg, Ma, and see if you can visualize her washing out a mouth with soap. If so, this should act as a cue to help you remember the third commandment.

Now let's memorize the remaining commandments. The sixth commandment states, "You shall not murder" (Exod. 20:13). Peg #6 is jaw or jawbone. Picture an angry man about to strike another man with a jawbone; then, put yourself into the picture and stop the murder by grabbing the jawbone. Commandment seven is "You shall not commit adultery" (Exod. 20:14). Key is the seventh peg, so in this case visualize a large key holding a bright flashlight. The key shines the flashlight on "a dull tree" (adultery). Because of the bright light, it is no longer a dull tree (no adultery).

"You shall not steal" is the eighth commandment (Exod. 20:15). Since peg #8 is ivy, let's picture a lush growth of green ivy completely enclosing and entangling a burglar. The burglar wears a mask over his eyes and lugs a large bag over his shoulder. The ivy prevents the burglar from stealing. The ninth commandment is "You shall not give false testimony against your neighbor" (Exod. 20:16). Bee is peg #9, so put a bee on a witness stand and place a Bible in his hand. The bee will not give false testimony now.

The tenth commandment warns "You shall not covet your neighbor's house . . . wife . . . or anything that belongs to your neighbor" (Exod. 20:17). Imagine a giant set of toes, peg #10, standing in your yard scrutinizing your neighbor's house with a pair of binoculars. Then picture another set of toes walking over, taking the binoculars, and putting a blindfold over the eyes of the first set of toes. This is the cue for not looking on or coveting your neighbor's possessions.

If you vividly imagined the mental pictures described to you, your mind now holds the Ten Commandments. To recall any commandment you need only remember your 10 pegs. For example, if you wish to recall the sixth commandment, just visualize the sixth peg, jawbone. The thought of the jawbone will, by association, automatically prompt the image of the murder scene that you imagined. You stopped the murder by grabbing the jawbone. This should be enough to remind you that the sixth commandment is "You shall not murder." Try another number from 1 to 10 and test your recollection of the Ten Commandments. If any are unclear, reviewing them a few times will help secure them in your mind.

This is how the peg system works. To the picture for each peg, you associate another picture; this second picture contains cues to remind you of the information that you wish to remember. To recall that information merely recall the picture of the peg. When you do, the picture of your cue automatically comes with it because the two are linked together in your mind.

The Rhyming Peg System

To some people sounds and rhymes are more striking than sights. The peg system can be modified to accommodate such people. Instead of using the number code to create pegs out of the numbers from 1 to 10, rhymes are employed. A rhyming peg system looks like this:

1 = bun	6 = sticks
2 = shoe	7 = heaven
3 = tree	8 = gate
4 = door	9 = sign
5 = hive	10 = hen

To use this system, simply visualize the information that

you wish to remember and associate it in a picture with one of the rhyming pegs. For instances, in the Ten Commandments instead of Ma washing out that naughty boy's mouth, just imagine a tree doing the washing. Your imagination can create either picture with equal ease. As long as tree means three to you, the rhyming peg system will work for you, too.

The peg system is a handy way to store and recall Bible information. It is easy and fun to use in everyday life as well. Picture giant eggs in a tea cup, Noah slicing some fresh bread, and Ma popping out of an enormous milk carton, and you have started to memorize a grocery list.

Applications of the peg system and the number code are limited only by the imagination. In Part III of this book you will learn how to use these memory aids to fill your mind with the Word of God.

CHAPTER SIX

Interest: Fuels the Memory Machine

Interest is critical to a good memory. It is the fuel, the energy that drives an active, alert mind. Without interest, boredom and fatigue set in. Little is remembered in this state. In contrast, good recall requires concentration, awareness, involvement, and attention. As Samuel Johnson noted, "The true art of memory is the art of attention."

You are obviously interested in God's Word, or you would not be reading this book. Nevertheless, how does one maintain or increase interest? Motive is the answer. The best place to begin is within. The greatest commandment is to "Love the Lord your God with all your heart and with all your soul and with all your mind" (Matt. 22:37). A deep abiding love of God and His Word will inspire you to seek Him, to know Him, and to please Him. According to Christ "where your treasure is, there your heart will be also" (Luke 12:34). Your motivation, your interest in treasuring God's Word, should ultimately reside in your heart.

Amidst all his suffering, Job still revered God enough to say, "I have treasured the words of his mouth more than my daily bread" (Job 23:12). What a beautiful testimony to the value of God's Word. It should inspire us to do the same. Filling your mind with His Word is a wonderful expression of your love and reverence for God. Alexander Pope, the poet, voiced this thought well when he said, "How vast a memory has Love!"

Keep Memorizing Fun

As your love for God grows, so will your joy. Interestingly, this joy and happiness will also improve your ability to learn and remember. A study by Dr. Gordon Bower of Stanford University revealed that when people learn new material while happy, they will recall it more easily when in that same happy mood (Begley and others 1986, 49). Similarly, most unpleasant memories fade with time, but pleasant memories live on in our minds. This facet of our memory is surely a blessing from God. So if you wish for your memory work to last, enjoy it.

In the Bible classes that I teach, I usually save memory work for the end of the class period. I generally quiz the students's recollection of our prior memory assignment and add a new assignment. We usually have fun, and I purposely create humorous memory aids to help them remember the material that we have covered. Together we enjoy the satisfaction of recalling so much more of our Bible study and usually leave the classroom in good spirits.

Because of the drudgery of the rote method, memorization has a stigma attached to it for many people. They associate memorization with countless drills and repetitions of their material. It is arduous and time-consuming labor with little charm to it. Others may fear memory work and doubt their ability to do it. This attitude generally stems from failures to successfully memorize or recall God's Word. This should not be so "for God did not give us a spirit of timidity, but a spirit of power, of love, and of self-discipline" (2 Tim. 1:7). God gave us all the mental skills and ability to recall His Word.

Perhaps one of the values of using memory aids such as those taught in this book is that they are both powerful and fun. This maintains interest and satisfaction. As you sense your powers of memory improve by applying the skills you learn here, savor your growth. Relish the ease with which you can remember God's Word, and of course thank Him for your new abilities. In whatever ways you can, continue to sustain your interest in remembering God's Word by keeping it enjoyable.

Employ All Your Senses

When you put positive emotions to work, you will naturally become more deeply involved in your Bible study. This involvement is essential. You can also increase your involvement by employing as many of your senses as possible with the material that you are studying. When you engage as many avenues of learning as you can, you automatically amplify your capacity to remember.

Memory experts frequently use and teach this technique of applying all the senses. Remembering a name is a good example. They teach that to remember the name of someone just introduced to you, you should: 1) listen attentively to the name (hearing), 2) say the name during your conversation (engage speech and hearing), 3) jot down the name afterwards (sight and touch), and 4) create a vivid mental picture of the name and associate it to the face (Lorayne 1975).

This memory technique applies to a variety of Bible study situations as well. In chapter 9 this technique and others will be used to help you remember sermons and Bible study classes.

Involving yourself in your Bible memorization can be achieved quite literally in your visualization techniques. When you create your vivid mental images as memory aids, include yourself in them as often as you can. Put yourself and your emotions in your mental pictures. Because your own actions are, by nature, more interesting and important to you than the actions of others, they are recalled more easily.

This holds true for your voice, too. Your mind is very attentive to the sound of your voice. Besides all the other memory techniques that you can apply, if you wish to recall something be sure to simply say it aloud.

Set Goals

Goals also stimulate interest and satisfaction, for God

created our minds to seek goals. Our principal goal is to know Him, a desire He planted deeply within us.

> From one man he made every nation of men, that they should inhabit the whole earth; and he determined the time set for them and the exact places where they should live. God did this so that men would seek him and perhaps reach out for him and find him, though he is not far from each one of us (Acts 17:26-27).

Thus the desire to seek God dwells in everyone. For some it is a burning desire, for others it merely smolders. Nevertheless, the desire to seek God is behind your quest to know and recall God's Word more perfectly. This is evident even in our language. The Greek word for man is "anthropos," which, among other things, means "the upward looking one." Yes, mankind is born to seek God. And surely He is not far from each of us, for in each man and woman lives the image of God (Gen. 1:26).

The goal-seeking nature of the mind of man is recognized in secular literature, too. Goals were an integral part of the self-help psychology espoused by Dr. Maxwell Maltz in his popular book Psycho-Cybernetics. Though not crediting God as the source, Dr. Maltz recognized that "Man is by nature a goal-striving being. And because man is 'built that way' he is not happy unless he is functioning as he was made to function — as a goal striver" (Maltz 1960, xv).

So set goals for your memory work; they are natural and important for your continued spiritual growth. Start with modest goals, such as memorizing single scriptures. Then take a chapter of the Bible and memorize all of its main topics. You might consider an entire book and memorize it chapter-by-chapter. All of these goals are well within your reach, particularly if you learn the techniques taught in this book.

Once you set goals, be determined to complete them. Half-completed projects will not further your Christian growth. What your Heavenly Father needs, what the world needs, are motivated Christians willing to strive to finish their goals. If you feel your resolve wane, just think of, or better yet, memorize Philippians 4:13, "I can do everything through him who gives me strength."

Get Organized

Once you have set goals, being organized will help you achieve them. Rather than leave your Bible study and memory work to chance, set a definite time and place to study your Bible. If you think most clearly in the morning, schedule some study time then. Perhaps you could get up a few minutes early and study before breakfast. The stillness of the morning hours is a perfect time to meditate on God's Word. There is certainly no finer way to begin the day than with prayer and Bible study. Perhaps you would rather close your day that way. Whatever your choice, it is essential to set aside a specific time and place to study and memorize. As you faithfully hold to your schedule, Bible study will become a pleasant and rewarding habit, one you will cherish with time, for you will slowly but surely fill your mind with the wonder of God's Word.

I heard a story once that illustrates the effectiveness of daily Bible study. In India a particular process is used to dye a piece of cloth so that it will be colorfast. The cloth is dipped in dye and then hung in the sun to dry. The next day the cloth is again immersed in the dye and dried in the sun. This process is repeated each day for many days. Slowly, steadily the dye permeates every fiber of that cloth until at last it is color-fast. Due to this process, its color will not fade or lose its brilliance.

Bible study operates in much the same way. As you immerse yourself daily in God's Word, your faith grows a little stronger with each session. In time the truth and beauty of God's Word will permeate every fiber of your being. The days, months, and years of communion with God through His Word will fashion in you a faith that is unshakable.

The Ultimate Goal: Reflect His Glory

Finally and most importantly, interest and involvement reach fruition as a Christian acts on his or her knowledge of God's Word. In fact, as you absorb more of God's Word into your mind, it will ultimately be reflected in your actions, for "the word of God is living and active" (Hebrews 4:12). It has the power to accomplish much and change lives. Just as God sends the rain and snow to nourish the earth, His word grows forth to accomplish His will:

> So is my word that goes out from my mouth: It will not return to me empty, but will accomplish what I desire and achieve the purpose for which I sent it (Isaiah 55:11).

As you treasure the Word of God in your heart and mind, you will mature and blossom as a Christian. Then will you fulfill the ultimate goal of remembering God's

Word: to be changed, to be transformed into a person after God's own heart. Joy will be yours as you fulfill 2 Corinthians 3:18:

> And we, who with unveiled faces all reflect the Lord's glory, are being transformed into his likeness with ever-increasing glory, which comes from the Lord, who is the Spirit.

CHAPTER SEVEN

Patterns: Reduce the Amount to be Memorized

Most of what you read or hear is structured; it has a pattern, a design, a framework. Recognizing that structure will increase your recall of the material by: 1) condensing the material into a smaller package, 2) increasing your comprehension of the information, and 3) improving your ability to locate specific items within the material. All three of these increase your recall, either directly or indirectly. Condensing the data into its structural components improves recall directly, simply by reducing the amount that you must remember in order to absorb the information into your mind. Perceiving the structure of the material naturally increases your comprehension of it. This indirectly improves your remembrance of the material, for increased comprehension typically increases recall. Good

Bible recall also requires locating information in your Bible as well as in your mind. Understanding the structure and organization of the Bible will improve your ability to locate information within it.

Reduce the Amount to be Memorize

Condensing material into its structural components or into its essential elements greatly reduces the amount of data that you must attempt to remember. For example, if you were enjoying a scene overlooking a beautiful forested area among mountains and valleys, how would you recall it? I doubt that you would try to remember each tree and each rock. Rather you would recall groves of trees, the general form of the mountains, and the pattern that the streams cut in the hillsides. Perhaps you would selectively recall a particularly tall or colorful tree or an outstanding outcrop of rock. These exceptional features would be recalled along with the general form of the landscape. This simplified impression is all that your mind needs to recall that vision at a later time.

The same process works in Bible memorization. Selecting the highlights and fitting them into the overall structure of the material reduces what you must memorize and still maintain accurate recall. Outlining is an excellent method for grouping material into common topics and selecting key points. To aid your recall of the Bible, it is beneficial to study outlines of the books that you are reading, and to construct your own outlines.

The process of reducing data by grouping similar items is called classification or simply "chunking." As the word implies, chunking means to group several items into a chunk. The chunk is then memorized in place of each item separately. When studying the Bible, look for common themes or topics to chunk. Those common or recurring themes are present if you look for them.

By identifying and remembering the main points of a Bible lesson, a scripture, or a chapter you will be surprised at how much more of the material you will also be able to recall. The main points or themes cue your remembrance of other portions of the material that you did not consciously try to store in your memory.

The mental process is similar to that of memorizing the first Beatitude. You established cues only for the nouns, verbs, and important descriptors, but your memory, using these words as cues, filled in the other words necessary to complete the verse. This occurs on a larger scale, too. If you memorize the main topics of a chapter in the Bible, as you will learn in chapter 11, you will be able to recite not only the main topics, but much of the fine detail as well. It is a wonderful God-given property of your mind. Just given a rough sketch of a picture, your mind quite naturally fills the canvas with color.

Increase Comprehension and Improve Recall

Your recall of material is also indirectly improved through the seeking of structure and patterns. When you scrutinize the structure of Bible material by selectively locating key teachings and principles, you automatically increase your comprehension of it. As a pleasant by-product, increased comprehension naturally increases recall.

The relationship between comprehension and recall is evident to anyone who has listened to a highly disorganized, rambling sermon. It was probably difficult to understand and to follow and certainly left little impression on your memory. On the other hand, a highly organized presentation is easier to follow and, therefore, easier to grasp and recall.

Understanding and comprehension enhance recall by increasing the number of associations that you can make with the new material. As you know, your learning and memory depend on making associations between what you wish to learn and what is already in your memory. If the Bible material that you are studying makes little sense to you, there are few associations that you can make between it and what you already know about the Bible. Therefore, tools that supplement your understanding of the Bible will improve your ability to form associations, which will ultimately improve recall.

One important supplement to comprehension and the discerning of structure is an understanding of the context of the Scriptures. This oftentimes requires reading books about the Bible to gain a better perspective of the times in which various portions of the Bible were written. A wealth of historical and archeological studies are available that will broaden your understanding of Biblical events.

Understanding the prophecies in the book of Daniel is a good example. Appreciating secular history and the succession of the kingdoms of Assyria, Babylon, Persia, Greece and Rome is invaluable in interpreting and remembering this book. Numerous associations can be created between historical kings and kingdoms and the prophecies of Daniel. Increasing the number of these kinds of associations to the material in Daniel will improve both your understanding and recall of the book.

Finally, seeking patterns and structure increases your involvement and interest in your subject matter. As you learned in the preceding chapter, this, too, increases the power of your memory. Seeking structure, looking for principle themes, searching for patterns, all these demand energy and concentration. While focusing your attention in this manner, the material is simultaneously impressed firmly in your memory.

Speed Your Search For Data

As you can see, discerning patterns indirectly augments recall. Discerning patterns and organization can aid your memory in another way: it can speed your recall of the correct location of information that you are searching for. Part of good Bible recall is knowing where to look for certain kinds of information, and knowing where to look is generally related to understanding the structure and context of the Bible. How often have you said, "I know that's in the Bible, but I just can't place where"? Many times the memory fails not in recalling information, but rather in failing to remember its location. A sound grasp of the Bible's organization will speed your search for data.

The four Gospels illustrate this point. Each author wrote his version of the life of Christ for a different reason. Matthew, a Jew, wrote to the Jews and portrays Jesus as the fulfiller of prophecy, the Messiah. Mark characterizes Jesus as a man of action and emphasizes His ministry and miracles. Luke, a Gentile, addressed primarily

Gentile Christians and features Christ as the Saviour of all mankind, both Jew and Gentile. John, the devout apostle of Christ's, explained his reason for writing in John 20:31, "But these things are written that you may believe that Jesus is the Christ, the Son of God, and that by believing you may have life in his name."

Knowing the reasons for writing each book of the Gospels expedites a search for information in them. For instance, where do you look for links between the Old and New Testaments, the fulfillment of prophecy? Matthew would be the first choice. Where do you go to capture someone's interest in the Bible by revealing the dynamic actions of Christ? Mark would be a good choice and is often used to spark interest in non-Christians. Thus, knowing the structure of the Gospels can improve your recall of the best place to locate particular topics and appropriate subjects within them. Of course this holds true for the entire Bible and emphasizes the need to understand more about its organization.

The Organization of the Bible

Fortunately the Bible is a well-organized book. On several levels there is a sense of order that, if appreciated, will enhance your Bible recall. The books of the Bible are grouped logically, by topic primarily. Individual books are usually well-structured, and even chapters are generally organized. Let's look first at the arrangement of the books in the Old and New Testaments.

Table 7-1 illustrates that the books of the Bible are ordered topically. The five books of the law, the Penta-

Table 7-1
The Topical Division of Books of the Bible

The Old Testament

Law
Genesis
Exodus
Leviticus
Numbers
Deuteronomy

History
Joshua
Judges
Ruth
1 & 2 Samuel
1 & 2 Kings
1 & 2 Chronicles
Ezra
Nehemiah
Esther

Poetry & Wisdom
Job
Psalms
Proverbs
Ecclesiastes
Song of Solomon

Major Prophets
Isaiah
Jeremiah
Lamentations
Ezekiel
Daniel

Minor Prophets
Hosea
Joel
Amos
Obadiah
Jonah
Micah
Nahum
Habakkuk
Zephaniah
Haggai
Zechariah
Malachi

The New Testament

The Gospels
Matthew
Mark
Luke
John

History
Acts

Letters of Paul
Romans
1 & 2 Corinthians
Galatians
Ephesians
Philippians
Colossians
1 & 2 Thessalonians
1 & 2 Timothy
Titus
Philemon
Hebrews

General Letters
James
1 & 2 Peter
1, 2 & 3 John
Jude

Prophecy
Revelation

teuch, are followed by the books of history. Poetry and wisdom literature are next. Last are the books of prophecy, the five major prophets followed by the 12 minor prophets. The New Testament books are topically arranged, too. They are arranged as follows: the Gospels, history, the letters of Paul, general letters, and prophecy.

Though different in Jesus' time, the order of the Old Testament books was still topical. Jesus referred to a topical three-fold organization when He said, "Everything must be fulfilled that is written about me in the Law of Moses, the Prophets, and the Psalms" (Luke 24:44). Individual books of the Bible are oftentimes well organized, too. The book of Job is a good example. Were you to begin reading Job without realizing its structure, it might appear rather chaotic and confusing. In chapter 1, God refers to Job as "blameless and upright" (Job 1:8); yet, within a few chapters Job is defending his integrity before three presumed friends, Eliphaz, Bildad, and Zophar. Job's speech is constantly interrupted by his three friends, who contradict and condemn him, and even contradict themselves at times.

Nevertheless, the book of Job has a definite structure that, if appreciated, helps you understand the book. Much of Job is a debate between Job and his three friends. After a prologue consisting of chapters 1 and 2 and an opening statement by Job in chapter 3, the two sides square off and hotly debate the issue of Job's righteousness. First Eliphaz speaks; then Job replies to his charges. Next, Bildad speaks, and again Job replies. Finally, Zophar argues his point, and Job responds. This forms the first cycle of speeches, which extends from chapters 4 to 14.

A second cycle of speeches, having the same format,

extends from chapters 15 through 21. The third and last cycle, minus a speech from Zophar, covers chapters 22 to 31. The book closes with speeches by an arbitrator of sorts, Elihu, (chapters 32-37) and God (chapters 38-42).

The role of the three friends as "devil's advocates" in a debate with Job explains their often contradictory statements. Appreciating this structure is essential to comprehending the book of Job, and as we have noted, increased comprehension indirectly improves recall. In addition, were you to try to memorize Job, the book could be simplified from 42 individual chapters into five groups of chapters: the first three introductory chapters, the three cycles of speeches, the speech of Elihu, and the speech of God. This grouping or chunking would reduce the amount of material that you would have to memorize to gain an overview of the book. How would you go about memorizing an entire book? You will learn that skill in chapter 11 of this book.

Patterns in Numbers

Sometimes patterns in the Bible are accidental, but nevertheless, quite useful. Did you know that Ephesians 2:14 and Colossians 2:14 discuss the same topic? Both scriptures affirm that Christ destroyed the division between Jew and Gentile by removing the Mosaic Law. Merely this pattern in the scripture reference, that the chapter and verse are identical, has inscribed this fact in my memory. Recognizing the same pattern has helped me to recall that Hosea 6:6 and Micah 6:6-8 both teach the value of mercy over sacrifice.

Similarly, because of the repeating pattern in the scripture references of Jeremiah 31:31, John 17:17, and Deuteronomy 29:29, I can recall the location of: 1) a prophecy concerning the New Covenant, 2) an affirmation that God's Word is truth, and 3) a statement that God revealed only certain things to man. My recall of these particular scriptures has been enhanced in two ways because of the pattern of the numbers. First, the pattern caught my attention, and two, I needed to remember just one number for both chapter and verse.

Other people use patterns in numbers to prompt their memories. A classic example is a man named Dario Donatelli who developed an exceptional recall for large numbers by recognizing patterns in them (McKean 1983, 28). He was able to memorize a 73 digit number in under two minutes, a world record. "His secret: as a devoted cross-country runner, he often relates groups of figures to various running times already fixed in his memory. . . By stringing together racing times, or even the dates of famous races, he finds he can remember long series of unrelated digits" (McKean 1983, 28).

You may not be a long-distance racer, but number patterns exist in the Bible that may mean something to you. Let me share one more example with you. To the mathematically inclined, 2 Corinthians 4:16 has a number pattern: 2, 2x2=4, 4x4=16. This pattern of 2, 4, 16, prompts my recall of the location in 2 Corinthians where we receive the following encouragement, "Therefore, we do not lose heart. Though outwardly we are wasting away, yet inwardly we are being renewed day by day."

I am sure that there are many more such number patterns in the Bible. If you look for the patterns, you will find them, and they will give you one more tool to help you remember God's Word.

Developing good Bible recall, then, requires not only the use of visualization, association, and interest; an effective memory is selective and seeks to identify the underlying structure and meaning of all new information.

Using the analogy of the beautiful forest scene that we discussed to begin this chapter, when surveying your Bible look for the tall timbers and the bold outcrops. If you constantly fix them in your memory, the panorama of the Bible will eventually unfold in your mind.

CHAPTER EIGHT

Review: How Much and How Often

Review is crucial to the long term recall of Bible knowledge. Without review even the best, most effective memory aids will fail. On the other hand, excessive review is inefficient and unnecessary. The rote process of memorization employs review and repetition to an extreme. If you wish to maximize your accumulation of Bible knowledge and recall, it is important to understand both how much review is necessary and when to review for optimum results.

How Much To Review

First let's discuss the optimum number of repetitions for

efficient review. Dr. Herman Ebbinghaus, a pioneer in memory studies, researched this problem and discovered an interesting and time-saving principle (Loftus 1980, 65-66). He found that he could learn the same material in less time if he spread his review over three days rather than squeezing it into one day. For example, he learned that to accurately memorize a series of random letters, 68 repetitions were required in one day. Nevertheless, if the repetitions were spread over three days, only a total of 38 repetitions were needed. Memorizing more difficult material, Ebbinghaus took "504 repetitions in one day, but needed only 158 times the first day, 109 times the second day, and 75 times the third day" (Furst 1972, 27). The total repetitions for three days was 342, about 30% less than the one day total of 504.

Before you become dismayed by the total number of repetitions, let me assure you that your situation will be very different. The material Ebbinghaus memorized had no meaning to him; it was just random sequences and groups of letters. The number of repetitions that you will need for effective review will be significantly fewer because the material that you study will have meaning. Furthermore, because of memory aids it will be vividly inscribed in your mind.

Though Ebbinghaus did not memorize the same type of material that you will, the principle that he discovered is still helpful. Therefore, one important rule of efficient review is to spread out the process over a number of days rather than into one "cram" session. You will save time this way and yet recall with equal proficiency. Although I have not systematically recorded the number of repetitions that I need to learn Bible material, rarely do I repeat things more than ten times at one sitting. Generally three to five reviews in one day followed by one to three more times in each of the next two days is sufficient to memorize what I am studying.

Often I spread my review over the whole day. I review a little in the morning, and then, during spare moments in the rest of the day, I sneak in a few more reviews. This contact with God's Word during the day uplifts me and re-centers my mind on spiritual matters. By reviewing my memory schemes on the commute home, I have transformed that trip into a pleasant communion with God's Word. In fact, every time that I pause to consider the Bible, my day is brightened. I recommend it to you, too. These little mental reviews during the day will help you fulfill an important scripture: "Set your minds on things above, not on earthly things" (Col. 3:2).

When to Review

Knowing that it is best to spread your review over a period of days rather than a single day, let's now examine which days are best for review. Again Ebbinghaus supplies an answer from his research. He established that most forgetting occurs in the three days following your first exposure to new material (Psychology Today 1972, 180-181). In fact over 50% of new material can be lost in just one hour after learning it! After a day about 70% of the material is lost and 30% is retained. Beyond three days very little additional material is lost.

The critical time to review is clear! The three days immediately following your initial study and especially that first day. For this reason at the end of every Bible class I generally remind my students to review their new memory aids on their way home or at least before going to bed. A quick review shortly after exposure to new material will pay large dividends later in better recall. If you have memorized a sermon that you have just heard, reviewing it on the way home will strongly reinforce it in your memory. After the first day's review, continue reviewing over the following two days using fewer repetitions (as we learn ed at the beginning of this chapter). Then continue spot checks of your recall over the next two weeks. If, after two weeks, your recall is sound and accurate, you will likely retain this new information for several months. If, after six months, a review reveals that you have lost a little, it is quite easy to refresh your memory and re-learn the lost information.

Review can assume different forms. As we have discussed, review may mean the repetition of items that you wish to memorize. This form of review applies particularly to the memorization that must be exact or word-for-word. Memorizing scriptures, or factual knowledge falls into this category; however, if the material does not need to be recalled verbatim, other forms of review are effective.

Restatement: A Powerful Form of Review

If you simply wish to recall the gist of a Bible lesson, a sermon, or a chapter, another form of review, called restatement, serves well. Restatement merely means to re-express what you have learned in your own words. You do not try to exactly reproduce the material; instead, you assess what you have learned and express it using your own thoughts and feelings.

Restating newly learned material powerfully impresses the information into your memory in several different ways. One is merely by the principle discussed in chapter 7; we attend to our own thoughts and constructions over those of others. Your conclusions and thoughts are naturally important and interesting to your mind. This heightens concentration and automatically increases recall.

Restating another's ideas in your own words also forces you to think more deeply about the ideas. It requires from you some analyses and perhaps some comparisons with your prior understanding of the topic, and it forces you to consciously process the new information. This processing produces better recall according to some memory researchers. In fact, some "psychologists think that 'depth of processing' is related to retention . . . studying words for their meaning brings more of the mind into play than mere attempts at memorization. Moreover, the improved recall lasts" (Begley and others 1986, 54). Restatement then, checks your understanding, reinforces meaning, and improves recall. It is indeed a powerful tool for review.

Your restatement may be written as well as verbal. A written restatement has one valuable advantage; it furnishes a permanent record of your learning. Written outlines are excellent forms of restatement that may be applied to a variety of material. Bible classes, sermons, chapters and even books of the Bible are good candidates for outlines. Your outlines will stimulate your recall and understanding now and be valuable review aids in the future.

Generate a Reading Record

Conscientiously outlining and condensing all that you read generates a "reading record." This, too, is a powerful memory tool. I was first introduced to a reading record when a job change required that I learn a new field of my profession. During two years I faithfully kept a written record of every technical article that I read, which totalled about 5,000 pages. After reading each article, I restated it, recording in my own words the thoughts, facts, or principles that I felt were significant. Each restatement was typed on an index card along with the article reference. This reading record proved invaluable and made the time that I spent reading far more useful to me.

This process could be easily applied to Bible reading. For every chapter or book that you read, why not save a written record of what you learned? Sow the seeds of recall now, and you will reap a harvest of Bible knowledge and remembrance in the future.

When should your restatement begin? According to Dr. Ebbinghaus's research about our rate of forgetting, restatement should immediately follow learning. You need not record your thoughts at that time; instead, merely review the material in your mind. Continue reviewing during the next two days in order to refine your restatement, and by the third day write it out. Following these steps will minimize forgetting and optimize your recall.

Usage: The Finest Form of Review

Perhaps the finest form of review is usage. Each time

you put your new-found Bible knowledge into action you are, in effect, reviewing it. So speak up in Bible class. If you remember a scripture that is applicable to the discussion, mention it to the class. In so doing you will reinforce this scripture in your memory, while helping your classmates. After all we are to "consider how we may spur one another on toward love and good deeds" (Hebrews 10:24). Your contribution might be just what someone needs.

Outside of church services and classes, opportunities abound to implement your Bible knowledge. One of the beauties of good Bible recall is that your Bible is confined no longer to your bookshelf or the end table; it lies open within your mind at all times. Therefore, seek ways to blend it into your daily thoughts and speech. Put your knowledge into motion and make your recall of the Bible's message come alive in your Christian life. Above all, reflect it in your actions and "let your light shine before men, that they may see your good deeds and praise your Father in heaven" (Matt. 5:16).

PART III
APPLYING YOUR MEMORY SKILLS

CHAPTER NINE

How to Remember Sermons and Bible Classes

Have you ever listened to a Bible lesson, thoroughly enjoyed it, and yet, realized about an hour later that you could recall very little of it? Can you recall the major points of the sermon that you heard last Sunday? If your recall of Bible sermons or lessons is not what it should be, relax; using the skills that you just learned in Part II, your remembrance of the spoken word will increase many times.

Listening to God's Word should illuminate our minds and enrich our lives; yet, oftentimes we fail to capture all the rewards offered by Bible lessons. Why is it so difficult to pay attention and remember the spoken word? The answer may surprise you, for poor listening is not due to some mental deficiency that must be overcome. On the contrary, listening is difficult be cause it does not tax your mind!

Studies have shown that "the average speaker talks about 200 words per minute, while a listener can process information at around 300-500 words per minute" (Burley-Allen 1982, 51). In other words, you can listen from 1 1/2 to 2 1/2 times as fast as people can talk. Because the mind is not pressed to keep up with the speaker, it tends to wander, which eventually destroys attention and, of course, recall. If mind wandering becomes a habit, your listening becomes lazy and weak like a muscle that is not exercised enough.

Active Listening

Fortunately this excess listen capacity can be re-directed to stimulate greater attention and recall. How? By using the extra time to engage in "active listening." Most people listen passively, merely attempting to absorb what is said. Active listening is dynamic and employs your mind fully in the communication process.

One of the best active listening techniques is to engage in mental interplay. This transforms a passive one-way communication into an active, though imagined, two-way communication. As you listen, pretend that you are conversing with the speaker. Silently ask questions, and of course, answer all the speaker's questions. Try to anticipate what the speaker will say next and analyze carefully all of his or her main points. Do you agree or disagree? Can you recall other scriptures or references that pertain to the topic being discussed? Surprisingly, you can do all this and still follow the speaker because of your excess listening capacity.

Mental interplay increases your involvement, interest, and depth of processing of the material presented. This quite naturally betters your recall of it, without even applying any other memory aids.

Active listening also incorporates mental reviews, restatements, and outlines. During the sermon or Bible class, periodically summarize the material in your mind. In your own words restate the major conclusions and recommendations. As you know, you will recall your own conclusions and constructions more easily than another's.

Generally a minister or Bible class teacher outlines the topic to be presented. In delivering the lesson, the speaker usually refers to the outline and relates to the audience the main points as they are discussed. An active listener tunes in to these main points and especially notes them. In fact you, the listener, can construct your own outline of the talk, and you can do it without pencil or paper. With a little help from some memory techniques, you can assemble an outline entirely within your mind, a mental outline.

Mental Outlines

Mental outlines are powerful memory aids that have proven their worth to me repeatedly. How are outlines forged in the mind? It is easy using the peg system taught in chapter 5. As the speaker makes each point, the listener associates it to a number in the peg system. The first point is associated to peg #1. The second point is associated to peg #2 and so on. An example from an actual sermon will help illustrate the technique.

I recently heard a sermon on Ephesians 4:29, which describes a Christian's speech:

> Let no unwholesome word proceed from your mouth, but only such a word as is good for edification according to the need of the moment, that it may give grace to those who hear (NASV).

According to the minister this verse emphasized four things about our speech: 1) what not to say — unwholesome words, 2) what to say — words that edify and build up, 3) how to say it — according to the need of the moment, and 4) why say it — to give grace to the hearer.

With the peg system all four of these points can be stored in the memory in a mental outline. Using the rhyming peg system of chapter 5, the pegs for points #1 through #4 are: "bun," "shoe," "tree," and "door." Now as the speaker makes each point simply create a mental image that captures the meaning of the point and associate the image to the appropriate peg.

The mental outline for the sermon on Ephesians 4:29 might be assembled as follows: Peg #1 is bun, so mentally picture a hamburger bun with a large mouth. As words appear out of the bun's mouth, he grabs them and pokes a hole in them; thus, he lets no "unwholesome word proceed" from his mouth. Peg #2 is shoe; so visualize a shoe speaking to people through a megaphone as he stacks them up into a human pyramid. The shoe is building them up, edifying them through speech.

Peg #3 is tree; a tree is speaking to a large group of clocks (symbolizing time) perched on the tree's knee (need). The tree is addressing the "need of the moment." Finally, peg #4 is door; so picture in your mind a door lending a hand to help someone to their feet who has fallen. The tree is extending grace or benefit to the listener.

In a real situation you would be creating these mental pictures as the speaker makes each point. Due to your excess listening capacity, you will be able to do this and still follow the lesson.

To review or recall this sermon some time later, merely picture a bun, a shoe, a tree, and a door, and the mental images and their meaning will easily come to mind. This technique works well when you do not have the time or opportunity to write your outline while listening. The mental outline, if reviewed properly, will be retained for some time and can always be written out later if it is especially meaningful to you. With mental outlines, you always leave a sermon or Bible class with a little more of God's Word firmly anchored in your mind.

Engage the Senses

As well as involving yourself in mental interplay, reviewing, and outlining, there are still other ways to be an active listener. To keep alert and stimulate recall, you should engage as many of your senses as possible. Obviously hearing is engaged, but what about sight? If the minister refers to or reads a scripture, immediately find it in your Bible and follow along. In addition to hearing a scripture, seeing a scripture etches it more deeply in your memory. This benefits you in other ways, too. Just by sheer repetition and constant exposure to the Scriptures, the habit of looking them up eventually rewards you with a superior recall of their wording and location.

Finding scriptures in the Bible keeps your body, your kinesthetic sense active, too. This may also help, through constant practice, to locate scriptures. If nothing else it stimulates alertness and prevents drowsiness.

If feasible, involve more of your sense of sight and touch by taking notes. Writing your notes and seeing the words reinforces them in your memory. When note taking, it is best to re-word the lesson material according to your understanding of it. Trying to copy exactly what is said will not be as productive. Instead, be selective and condense the material into its essential elements. Mulling over the material for important points increases your depth of processing, which will increase your comprehension and recall.

If the Bible class employs discussion rather than strictly lecture, actively participate in the discussions, for this also increases your memory of it. Your mind is tuned to the sound of your voice and pays special attention to it. Thinking about what you will say, saying it, and hearing your own words will all reinforce the content of the lesson. Even if you do not answer a question aloud, always formulate a response in your mind. You can do this and still hear another's answer because of your excess listening capacity.

Review

Discussing topics outside of the class is also beneficial, for it maintains interest and increases retention. Discussions immediately after class are particularly useful because, as you learned in chapter 8, 40% of forgetting usually occurs within an hour after learning new material. Talking about the class material is a convenient way to review. The discussion need not be lengthy; a few words on the drive home from church provide sufficient review.

Regardless of the types of memory techniques that you employ to remember sermons and Bible classes, proper review optimizes the long-term recall of your new knowledge. In the two to three days following a sermon or class, review your mental outlines. Writing them would also be beneficial. If you took notes, review them and add details as they spring into your mind. I believe that you will be pleasantly surprised by your mental outlines and written notes, for they will cue many more details about the subject that you did not realize were stored in your memory. By the power of association, these extra details are drawn out by reviewing the outlines and notes.

The Benefits of Good Listening Habits

Good listening habits will speed your spiritual growth and improve your effectiveness in everyday life as well, for we spend more time listening than we spend talking, reading, or writing. According to studies of our communication tendencies, the average person spends about 40% of the time listening, 35% talking, 16% reading, and 9% writing (Burley-Allen 1982, 2). Listening, then, is the most important communication skill that you can possess.

Listening to God's Word is especially important, and throughout the Bible God appeals to man to "Hear the word of the Lord" (Isa. 1:10, 66:5, Jer. 7:2, 10:1, 19:3,

29:20, Mic. 6:1). The next time that you attend a sermon or Bible class, I hope that you will say in your heart, "I will listen to what God the Lord will say" (Ps. 85:8). I hope, too, that this chapter has inspired you to not only listen to the Word of God, but to remember it and act on it as well. If you do this, God will surely bless your life just as He has promised in James 1:22-25:

> Do not merely listen to the word, and so deceive yourselves. Do what it says. Anyone who listens to the word but does not do what it says is like a man who looks at his face in a mirror and, after looking at himself, goes away and immediately forgets what he looks like. But the man who looks intently into the perfect law that gives freedom, and continues to do this, not forgetting what he has heard, but doing it — he will be blessed in what he does.

CHAPTER TEN

How to Read the Bible for Greater Recall

Quiet moments immersed in Bible reading are truly precious. By drinking deeply from the Word of God, we commune with Him and grow in knowledge. Reading the Bible should be a time for renewal and growth, and if we read with greater understanding and recall it surely will be.

Of the two kinds of Bible reading, light devotional and in-depth, this chapter focuses on learning and recalling while engaged in in-depth reading. Many of the techniques and principles taught in the previous chapter about listening apply to reading, too. In reading, however, you control the flow of information. You can vary your reading rate and even stop if necessary. This control lightens the task of comprehending and recalling the study material.

Although it is possible to read at a rate near your limits

of comprehension, it is best to read at a slightly slower rate. This allows you to employ the techniques of active listening in order to become an "active reader."

Active Reading

As in active listening, an active reader engages in mental interplay. Building associations through mental interplay is particularly helpful. Compare the text that you are reading with passages in the Bible that cover related topics; this establishes associations of similarity. If you do this repeatedly, the harmony and unity of God's message will become increasingly evident, and you will create in your mind a filing system of scriptural topics and their location in the Bible.

Another useful memory tool employed in mental interplay is pattern seeking or classifying. Most scriptures can be classified as either: 1) A promise from God, 2) A commandment to keep, 3) A timeless principle, or 4) An application of a principle. As you read, classify the text according to one of the four groups above. This process clarifies your understanding of the text and at the same time plants one more link or association to prompt recall of the material later.

Finally, inject questions into your mental interplay. Questioning stirs interest and involvement, which you know is critical to memory. Imitate a good newspaper reporter and be inquisitive. Ask who, what, when, where, why and how? The deeper you dig into the Bible the greater the treasure you will uncover. As Christ promises in Matthew 7:7, "Ask and it will be given to you; seek and you will find; knock and the door will be opened to you."

Pause and Restate

Because you are reading and not listening you may stop at any time. If your mental interplay and questioning reveal that you do not comprehend the material, stop immediately and re-read the text. Even if you comprehend the text, periodically stopping for a quick review is an excellent memory strengthening habit.

After reading a paragraph, a half of a chapter, or a full chapter, pause, set down your Bible, and restate in your own your words what you have just learned. Start by describing the details of the text, the who, what, where, why, when, and how's. If these are fairly clear, think next about the meaning behind the facts. Consider the principles taught and applications for daily living. Because you are reading for greater recall and not for speed, take your time and draw out as much detail and interpretation as you can. If practical, you may wish to say aloud your restatement. The extra effort required to convert thoughts into speech will also impress the material more firmly in your memory.

If you experience difficulty recalling the text that you have just read, read shorter portions of it between restatements. Perhaps reading a half a chapter or a paragraph at a time would be better for you than a whole chapter. As you practice periodic reviews and restatements, you will learn how far to read between stops. I hope that you will use this technique. Though it slows your reading rate, if you mull over God's Word this way, you will increase your depth of processing, improve your comprehension, and strengthen your recall.

Highlight and Annotate Your Bible

God's Word is often called the "Holy Bible." The words of the Bible are holy indeed, but the paper it is printed on is not. Though I once shuddered at the thought of marking my Bible in any way, I now see the value in it. When I read technical articles in my profession, I generally highlight significant points in yellow and annotate the margins with thoughts or interjections of my own. This has proven so useful in recalling technical articles that I recommend it in Bible reading, too.

Highlighting and margin notes increase recall in several ways. As discussed in chapter 7 on patterns, scrutinizing the Bible for its organization and central principles improves comprehension and recall. This is exactly what is accomplished by highlighting important points. It forces the mind to evaluate all the material and select the most significant. It boils down or distills the material into its essentials and reduces the amount of data that must be stored in your memory.

Margin notes are another form of restatement. Instead of a verbal restatement, your margin notes comprise a written record of it. The notes need not always be words. Because the mind recalls pictures with startling ability, consider drawing small maps, pictures, or diagrams that help to capsulize what the Bible is saying.

Margin notes and color highlights enhance memory in another way; they speed review. The easiest and quickest method to review material that you have read is to merely re-read your margin notes and your color highlights. These are the items that are important to you, the ones that need to be recalled; therefore, review should naturally be focused on them. I believe that you will find this to be a convenient and effective form of review.

All Bibles are not suited for highlights and margin notes. An expensive reference Bible is already extensively annotated. You might be understandably hesitant to mark and color it. Instead, use an un-annotated Bible with large pages and wide margins. Of all the Bibles that I own, I am most fond of the dog-eared, marked, and highlighted one with which I have spent so many pleasant hours.

Outline Your Reading

To gain maximum benefit from your reading, you may wish to outline what you read. Just as mental outlines are invaluable memory aids in listening situations, written outlines optimize your long-term recall of Bible readings. A written outline is beneficial because it will force you to classify, condense, and restate the material that you have read. If, while reading, you have engaged in mental interplay, highlighted meaningful passages, and made margin notes, the ingredients for a good outline are already at hand. To outline the chapter or book that you have been reading merely review your highlights and margin notes. In addition, call upon the memory of your periodic restatement, and record the points that are especially significant to you. Then organize and record your thoughts into a written outline.

Outlines will impress your Bible reading firmly into your memory and prove invaluable whenever you wish to review. As revealed in chapter 8, a written reading record will yield fruit for many years. In essence, the reading record is your personal Bible commentary, and if you regularly and faithfully record all your Bible readings, your commentary will grow quite large. Your knowledge and recall of the Bible will naturally grow with your commentary. It will become a wonderful place to store the treasures of God's Word.

Read Books About the Bible

Finally, greater recall of Bible reading hinges on a sound understanding of the material. The amount recalled will increase in direct proportion to the amount understood. For this reason it is helpful to supplement your Bible reading with other books that amplify your comprehension of the Bible. Because many books are available to help you read the Bible with greater comprehension, I will just suggest a few things here.

One key to greater comprehension is context. Understanding the context of a book, a chapter, or even a verse of the Bible is crucial to an accurate understanding of its meaning. Before reading a book of the Bible, consult a Bible dictionary or other general reference to gain background information. Discover something about the author, his purpose, his audience, the historical setting, and the spiritual setting. Study an outline of the book and form a conceptual road map of the territory it will cover.

This preview prepares your mind to receive the meaning of your particular Bible reading. It primes your memory, too, for all learning and recall is founded on associations. If your mind already holds some preliminary information about the portion of the Bible that you are about to read, it will digest and store what you read with greater ease.

Preliminary study before reading is like preparing soil before planting. Because a well-prepared soil will yield more harvest than poorly prepared soil, it is important to prepare your mind before planting the Word of God in it. In the parable of the sower Jesus taught the value of good soil (Matt. 13:1-9, 18-23).

> This is the meaning of the parable: The seed is the word of God (Luke 8:11). What was sown on good soil is the man who hears the word and understands it. He produces a crop yielding a hundred, sixty, or thirty times what was sown (Matt. 13:23)

It is my hope that this chapter will help you to produce many-fold for Christ.

CHAPTER ELEVEN

How to Memorize Bible Chapters and Books

In the prior chapter you learned techniques to help you read the Bible with greater recall and understanding. Applying these techniques to your Bible reading will enable you to remember many of its major points, and you might even recall some of its fine detail. In this chapter you will go a step further in memory training; you will learn how to remember, in proper sequence, each significant event or principle discussed in any chapter of the Bible. You can choose the amount of information that is memorized, varying the detail from just the major points to a thought-by-thought recall of the entire chapter.

Learning a chapter thought-by-thought enables you to recite from memory the entire chapter in your own words. In addition to paraphrasing the chapter, you will probably be able to recite some of it word-for-word.

This may sound a bit farfetched; yet, it is well within your ability. Combining your natural powers of visualization, as sociation, and chaining will greatly reduce the difficulty of this task. In fact, you will be pleasantly surprised by the number of Bible chapters that you can file in your memory. Ironically, one of your greatest joys in Bible study may come when you close your Bible. For using the techniques taught here, you can close your Bible, open your memory, and read the Bible from your mind.

The Psalmist wrote, "I have hidden your word in my heart, that I might not sin against you" (Ps. 119:11). With a little study and effort, you too, can hide the Word of God away in your heart, and it will be with you wherever you go.

Memorizing a Chapter Step-by-Step

Memorizing a chapter of the Bible is a step-by-step process. The first step is to read the entire chapter using the techniques discussed in chapter 10; this provides an overview of the chapter and primes your memory with some of its significant topics and events. The second step is to re-read the chapter slowly, jotting down the items that you wish to remember in the order that they appear. If your Bible splits the text into paragraphs, use these divisions to consolidate or group several verses into one or two thoughts. The amount of detail that you list for memorization is your choice. With practice you will discover what level of detail satisfies you.

After listing the items to be memorized, the third step is

to convert each item into a mental picture. Concrete items are easily pictured; however, you may need to create some imaginative associations to transform abstract items into pictures. In addition to making pictures for the chapter's content, devise a mental image for the chapter's location. Use the number code of chapter 5 to transform the chapter's number into a picture. For instances, to memorize Mark 6, which you will do shortly, you might picture a large black felt marker (Mark) with a giant jawbone (6) sticking out of it.

Step four involves connecting your mental pictures together in an imaginative, humorous, colorful, and interesting way. Starting with the chapter location picture, fuse together the images containing the chapter's content in the order in which they appear. At the end of your string of images, tack on the chapter location image again.

The mental pictures that you create from the linked images contain the cues that will remind you of the content of the chapter. As you practice this method, I believe that you will amaze yourself. The amount of detail from a chapter that can be stored in the memory in this manner is truly astonishing.

Step five is that all-important process of review. Although your recall of interesting visualizations is quite strong, review implants the pictures and the meaning even more firmly in your mind. Rehearse the chapter's images several times immediately after you create them. Then, in the two or three days that follow, review them several more times. After a week, review the images again. By this time they should be fairly easy to recall, and you should probably start memorizing another chapter. Thereafter, periodically check your remembrance of the chapters that you have memorized and reinforce the weaker, more difficult images to recall.

Memorizing Mark 6

Before going any further, let's memorize Mark 6 to illustrate how the method works. To make this example easier, I am going to condense the chapter into just seven highlights. These seven highlights cover the major events of Mark 6. Memorizing these events in order will give you an excellent recall of the content of this chapter of Mark.

In order to distinguish this chapter from others that you memorize, it must be uniquely identified. The obvious and most useful method of identifying the chapter is its location in the Bible, in this case the sixth chapter of Mark. Therefore, the first image in your mental picture should remind you of Mark 6. Let's visualize a large cylindrical black felt marker to symbolize Mark, and using the number code for 6, which is jaw, let's stick a giant jawbone in the end of the marker. Now you have Mark 6.

The first event in Mark 6 is the return of Jesus to his hometown (v.1-6); however, because "in his own house a prophet is without honor" (Mark 6:4), Jesus performs few miracles there. The main elements of this event are Jesus, His hometown, and a prophet without honor. To prompt your recall of these elements mentally picture your home (hometown) balanced on top of the jawbone. Put a cross (a symbol for Jesus) and a dollar sign (profit = prophet) on the door of your home. Now picture this scene in your mind as vividly as possible.

Once this image is placed in your mind's eye, it can be easily recalled due to the power of your visual memory. As you recall the image, due to the powers of association you will link the images to their meaning relative to Mark 6.

In verses 7-13, Jesus sends out the Twelve to preach in the surrounding cities. To condense this event into a single image, picture a green traffic light (meaning go) with a numeral "12" (the Twelve disciples) painted on it. This traffic light is jutting out of the chimney of your home. This mental image should be sufficient to remind you that Jesus sent out the Twelve after leaving his hometown.

The third event is the tragic murder of John the Baptist by Herod (v.14-29). This story is naturally vivid and memorable; therefore, only a small cue is really needed to represent it. To me the most startling and graphic image of the story is the platter holding the head of John the Baptist. Visualize, then, a platter balancing on the top of the traffic light. On the platter place the head of John. If the identity of the head on the platter is unclear to you, picture a man on it taking a bath (Baptist) while yawning (yawn = John).

In verse 30, the Twelve return to Jesus and report on their work. To represent this visually, just see the platter roll off the traffic light, make a large curve, and return to a cross. This should cue you to the return of the Twelve.

The next significant event in Mark 6 is the feeding of the 5,000 (v.31-44). Jesus satisfies everyone's hunger with just five loaves of bread and two fish. Because this, too, is an interesting and easily visualized story, just a few visual cues will help recall it. Let's mentally picture the platter continuing to roll until it crashes into five giant loaves of bread standing on end as columns. The loaves support two fish that lie on top of them. This should remind how Jesus fed the 5,000. The five loaves may even help you to remember that five thousand were fed.

After feeding the 5,000, Jesus made his disciples board a boat and leave for Bethsaida, while He remained behind to pray. Later in the evening, He came to them walking on the water (v.45-52). To convert this story into a mental picture, imagine that a boat is on top of the two fish, and within the boat a large shoe is rowing. Also picture water gushing out of the shoe. The boat, the rowing, the shoe, and the water, should help you recall that while His disciples were struggling to row the boat, Jesus walked to them on the water.

In the final scene of Mark 6, Jesus and His disciples come ashore at Gennesaret. People from throughout the region flock to Jesus and are healed by merely touching Him (v.53-56). To translate this into the mental picture, visualize a cross (Jesus) popping out of the shoe and walking on the shore. See many ill people touch the cross and immediately become well.

To complete the memorization of Mark 6, tack on the chapter location to the end of the mental picture. In this case picture the cross touching a black felt marker and turning it into a giant jawbone.

Why place the chapter location at the end, too? It helps locate scriptures in the Bible. For example, let's assume that you have memorized all 16 chapters of Mark, and that you wish to find the story about the feeding of the 5,000. Feeding the 5,000 will conjure up the image of the five loaves of bread standing on end supporting two fish, but where is found in Mark? To place the event in the correct chapter, merely complete the string or chain of images that follow the bread loaves, and you will be led to the end of the chapter and its identity, Mark 6.

This memory aid for recalling Mark is displayed in Table 11-1 for your review. I believe that you will enjoy this form of Bible memorizing, and I am sure that you will be pleasantly rewarded for your efforts.

Memorizing a Book of the Bible

Of course the next step is to memorize a whole book, and now that you know how to memorize a chapter, memorizing a book is not so intimidating. To memorize a book simply establish a visual memory aid for each chapter just as you did for Mark 6. Label each memory aid with its corresponding chapter and number, and you will have a whole book of God's Word in your memory. That is a great feeling, one that I hope you will experience many times.

During a Bible study class of mine, we examined the book of Mark and created memory aids for each chapter. The combination of reading, studying, discussing, and memorizing was instrumental in inscribing the book of Mark on our minds. Now, by drawing on those visual memory aids, we can locate within Mark most of the major events in the life of Jesus. Besides being able to rapidly locate references in the Bible, the hours of Bible study were effectively spent, for we have stored much of God's Word in our minds. Furthermore, it was stored in such a way as to be easily recalled.

Table 11-1 Memorizing Mark 6

The Mental Picture	The Meaning
1. A black felt marker has a large jawbone sticking out of its top.	Mark 6
2. Sitting on top of the jawbone is your home with a cross and a $ sign on the door.	v.1-6, Jesus visits his home town. Does only a few miracles because "in his own house a prophet is without honor."
3. Jutting out of the chimney is a large traffic light with #12 painted on it and a bright green light shining.	v.7-13, Jesus sends his 12 disciples to go to preach and heal.
4. A platter is balancing on the top of the traffic light. On the platter is the head of John the Baptist.	v.14-29, Herod kills John the Baptist and has his head put on a platter.
5. The platter rolls off the light and makes a large turn toward home.	v.30, The disciples return.
6. The platter continues to roll and crashes in to 5 giant loaves of bread standing on end. Two fish lie on top of the loaves.	v.31-44, Jesus feeds the 5,000 with 5 loaves and 2 fish.
7. On top of the bread and fish is a boat with a large shoe rowing in it. Water is gushing out of the shoe.	v.45-52, The disciples leave in a boat without Jesus. He comes to them walking on the water.
8. A cross pops out of the shoe and walks on the shore. People from all over touch the cross and are healed.	v.53-56, After coming ashore Jesus is recognized. Many sick people from the surrounding area are healed by touching Him.
9. The cross touches a black felt marker and turns it into a giant jawbone.	Mark 6

Adding More Detail

Perhaps you wish to memorize more detail than we did in our example of Mark 6. To do so you only need to add more images to your mental pictures of the chapter. Using the first six verses of Mark 6 as an illustration, let me show you how to add detail. Turn your Bible to Mark 6:1-6, and follow along as you work through this illustration.

Begin the same way, picturing a black felt tip marker with a jawbone sticking out of it. On top of the jawbone is your home. Now visualize a cross and several other men walking into your home. This represents verse 1, where Jesus visits "his home town, accompanied by his disciples." Next, visualize a bathtub coming out of the front door. The bathtub has a sad face painted on it (Sad bath = Sabbath). A cross stands within the bathtub and is drawing on a chalkboard (teaching). Associate these images with Jesus teaching in the synagogues on the Sabbath. Picture the cross drawing a maze (amaze) on the chalkboard to symbolize that "many who heard him were amazed" (v.2).

A crowd gathers around the cross and draws a large question mark on the chalkboard. The crowd points to a carpenter (a man with a hammer in his hand) and to Mary, who is holding a bright, yellow sun (son). Mary's children surround her. This scene is to remind you that the people questioned the power of Jesus because they were familiar with His family. They said, "Isn't this the carpenter? Isn't this Mary's son?" (v.3) They mentioned Jesus' brothers and sisters, too. Also picture in your mind the people holding their noses in the air in disgust. This is to signify that "they took offense at him" (v.3).

Now see the crowd going to the front door of your home and removing a dollar sign ($ = profit = prophet) and throwing it to the ground. This will remind you of that famous quote by Jesus, "Only in his home town, among his relatives and in his own house is a prophet without honor" (v.4).

The cross then steps out of your home and moves among a large crowd of sick people. With one hand he touches just a few of them and heals them. With his other hand, He draws a maze around the word "faith" written in small letters on a chalkboard. Associate this mental picture to the fact that Jesus did no miracles there "except lay his hand on a few sick people and heal them. And he was amazed at their lack of faith" (v.5).

For the last verse, visualize the cross walking out of the crowd pushing the chalkboard, which is on wheels. The cross pushes it from village to village. This finishes verse 6, which relates that Jesus went teaching from village to village.

If you have faithfully pictured these images in your mind's eye as vividly as possible, you will now be able to very closely paraphrase all the detail of Mark 6:1-6. You might even be able to repeat some of it word-for-word. The remainder of Mark 6 could be memorized verse by verse in much the same way.

Don't be concerned by the number of images that would be necessary to remember in detail all of Mark 6. Because you are using the chain system to link one image to the next, almost an indefinite number of images can be stored this way. You do not have to recall all the images at one time; instead the chain system is constructed so that if you can recall one item in the chain, the next one will automatically appear in your mind. Thus, one by one, you are able to recall the entire chain of images.

All you need to start the process of recall is the first image, which is easy because it is the location image for Mark 6. After recalling that image, the rest of the chapter will appear in your mind just as you stored it, one image at a time. This is indeed a remarkable property of the mind, and one that is God-given.

The techniques taught in this chapter will truly help you memorize chapters and books of the Bible. Of all the memory methods that I have used to recall God's Word, this method has yielded the most satisfaction and spiritual growth. When you have memorized God's Word in this way nothing can separate you from it. The Bible is always at your call ready to come alive when you need it. Whether in a crisis or simply during some idle moments, anywhere, at anytime the Word of God is before you.

Perhaps you will be able to say as David did in Psalm 119:97, "Oh, how I love your law! I meditate on it all day long."

CHAPTER TWELVE

How to Memorize Scriptures Word-for-Word

Throughout Part III, you have progressively added greater detail and accuracy to your memorization. In chapter 9, the goal was recalling the main points and topics of a Bible class or sermon. Rather than a word-for-word recall, your learned how to recall the new material using you own words, a process called restatement. Chapter 10 taught greater recall when reading the Bible. Again, the goal was to store in your memory an accurate, capsulized summary of the reading's content expressed in your own words.

The emphasis shifted in chapter 11, where you learned how to store Bible chapters and books in your memory such that you could paraphrase them and even repeat some parts verbatim. Now let's tackle the memorization of scriptures. Here the goal will be a word-for-word recall, and although the goal has changed, the same memory techniques that you have been using will still apply.

The primary techniques for memorizing scripture are association, visualization, and chaining, the skills taught in chapter 4. You will also need to convert some abstract concepts into concrete symbols and to translate the numbers of scripture citations into pictures by in the number code system of chapter 5.

Although you wish to memorize each word of a scripture, each word does not need to be mentally pictured. Capitalizing on your natural instinct to seek patterns and group-related items, a scripture can be simplified into its major clauses and phrases for easier memorization. Identify and recall the key nouns and verbs of each clause, and the remainder of the words will generally follow. As you have seen before, given sufficient cues the mind automatically fills in the rest of the detail. This is true even of memorizing verbatim. The best way to teach you the process of memorizing a scripture is to show you; so let's do some examples!

Memorizing Luke 10:27

We will start with an easy one, Luke 10:27:

> 'Love the Lord your God with all your heart and with all your soul and with all your strength and with all your mind'; and, 'Love your neighbor as yourself.'

This scripture is relatively simple to memorize for two reasons. One, you have probably heard it many times. It is Jesus' powerful answer to the questions, "what must I do to inherit eternal life?" (Luke 10:25b) and "Of all the commandments, which is the most important?" (Mark 12:28b). Judging by the significance of these questions, this is a good scripture to memorize anyway, if you have not already done so.

Luke 10:27 is also easy to memorize because of its pattern, the repetition of the phrase, "with all your." Memorizing that phrase and the sequence heart, soul, strength, and mind will remind you of over half of the scripture.

Let's start with the scripture location, Luke 10:27. To mentally picture "Luke," change it into "luck," and then associate luck with a four-leaf clover. The number "10" translates into "toes," and 27 into "neck." Therefore, to visualize Luke 10:27, imagine yourself in a field full of clover; giant four leaf clovers sprout up between your toes and grow all the way up to wrap around your neck.

Then picture yourself, clover and all, hugging (love) a throne (God) sitting on the word "Lord." This symbolizes "Love the Lord your God." Now visualize yourself piling items on the seat of the throne. First you place a beautiful red "heart"; then take the sole (soul) off your shoe and put it on the heart. Next, set a heavy weight-lifting barbell (strength) on the sole. Finally place on the barbell a mortar board similar to what you wore for graduation. This represents "mind." Now you have the order for the repeating phrase, "with all your heart . . . soul . . . strength . . . mind." After you've placed the mortar board, picture hugging your neighbor and then hug yourself. That's all there is to it.

Now to recall the verse, merely start with the thought, Luke 10:27. This should summon the first image, that of the four-leaf clover, the toes, and the neck. Once you have this first image in mind, the rest will follow one by one like links of a chain. Each succeeding image will remind you of the nouns, verbs, and other important words in the verse. These, in turn, will help you to recall the remaining words of the verse. Try it now, and see how it works.

Visualization Verses Rote Memorization

Memorizing Luke 10:27 was easy for you I hope, and perhaps you are wondering if all that visualization is really necessary. After all, many people have successfully memorized scripture by the rote method, which involves many repetitions of the verse to be remembered. Although the rote method works, I believe that even word-for-word memorizing using association, visualization, and chaining is generally quicker and more permanent.

It is quicker because you spend less time repeating the scripture. After analyzing the scripture a few times to establish your mental images and associations, only a few reviews of the verse and visualizations are necessary. Fewer reviews are necessary because the scripture is now stored in your visual memory, which is far superior to your memory for words. Your recall of the scripture will be more permanent for the same reason. Just as you can recall a face but not a name after many years have passed, you will be able to recall and recognize the meaning of the visualizations that you use to memorize scriptures.

Memorizing Micah 6:8

Let's practice the system again by memorizing Micah

6:8 word-for-word:

> He has showed you, O man, what is good. And what does the Lord require of you? To act justly and to love mercy and to walk humbly with your God.

This scripture has almost the same number of words as Luke 10:27, but is more difficult to learn because it is less well known. Nevertheless, a pattern in Micah 6:8 simplifies the memorization. The infinitive "to" is repeated in "to act," "to love," and "to walk." Noting this pattern will streamline the memorizing process.

As always start with the scripture location. If you still recall (and I hope that you do!) the order of the Minor Prophets taught in chapter 3, then you recall that Micah was pictured as "My Car." Begin by mentally picturing "My Car," which of course should be your own car. In the front seat place the chapter number, which is six, or jaw according to the number code. Therefore, imagine a large jawbone driving My Car. In the back seat place the number for the verse, which is eight or ivy. So picture lush vines of ivy growing in the back seat and out of the windows.

The ivy wraps around a large throne that is sitting on top of your car. The word "HE" in capital letters is sitting on the throne. This reminds you that the "HE" that starts the verse refers to God (the throne). The throne has arms and is using them to show a movie. The light of the movie projector shines through a large circular hoop, an "O," which is held by a man. This symbolizes, "He has showed you, O man." The light from the movie projector shines on a screen and reveals a light bulb (a symbol for watt = what) and the word, "GOOD," written in large capital letters. This should serve as a cue for the second clause, "what is good."

The next line of the verse begins with "And." Because first words are important cues that help you to recall the remainder of a phrase or clause, include a mental image of the beginning word when memorizing verbatim. To recall "And" substitute the sound alike, "ant." Therefore, start the second line by imagining a large ant taking the light bulb off the movie screen. This is the symbol for "And what." Now picture the ant placing the light bulb on a throne sitting on the word "Lord." The throne extends its arms to a large letter "U" as if asking or requiring some thing of the "U." These mental images are designed to stimulate the recall of "And what does the Lord require of you."

Although it takes many words to explain these images to you, it takes only a few moments to imagine them. When your begin to construct your own mental images, the process will be much quicker.

The third and final sentence of the verse starts with "To." Let's use a large numeral "2" to represent this and dress the "2" as a Shakespearean actor. The actor carries a large wooden judge's gavel (justice). This signifies "to act justly." The actor-numeral drops the gavel (on an ant if you wish to remember the connective word "and") and hugs a heart, which walks by. The heart has the word "mercy" inscribed on it. This means "to love mercy." Finally the numeral-actor watches a throne walk past him and follows behind the throne with head bowed low. Associate this with "to walk humbly with your God."

Now you've memorized Micah 6:8. Review the mental images once or twice and associate them to the words of

Micah 6:8. With just a little practice and review I am sure that you will be able to recite the verse verbatim.

Memorizing Joshua 24:15

One last example should illustrate the power of visualization in scripture memorization. Let's memorize Joshua 24:15, a more complex verse of 53 words:

> But if serving the Lord seems undesirable to you, then choose for yourselves this day whom you will serve, whether the gods your forefathers served beyond the River, or the gods of the Amorites, in whose land you are living. But as for me and my household, we will serve the Lord.

What a beautiful expression of Joshua's faith. It was a stirring challenge to the people of Israel to choose between worshipping idols or serving God, who had faithfully given them the Promised Land of Canaan. Regardless of the people's decision, though, Joshua's choice was clear; he and his household would serve the Lord. This courageous stand is well worth memorizing!

Joshua is famous for the fall of Jericho's walls from the blast of the trumpets (Joshua 6); therefore, mentally picture Joshua as a man holding a trumpet. The chapter number, 24, translates into "n" (2) and "r" (4), which can be used to spell "Nero," the infamous Roman emperor who fiddled while Rome burned. The verse is 15, which translates into "doll" (d=1 and l=5). So to picture the location of this memory verse, imagine that Joshua blows a man with a fiddle (Nero) out of his trumpet. Nero, in turn, plays his fiddle with a doll rather than a bow.

Because of that important first word in the verse, let's form a vivid image for "But." I suggest a cigarette butt. To connect the location image to the beginning word, imagine the doll throwing a cigarette butt to the ground. The butt dresses as a butler and, carrying a tray, walks up to a throne, our symbol for God or Lord. The butler notices a seam (seems) on the throne and turns abruptly away holding his nose up in apparent disgust (undesirable). These mental images convey the first phrase, "But if serving the Lord seems undesirable to you."

Next imagine that the butler, while carrying four large blocks of cheese (choose for), walks through a giant paper calendar (this day). He walks through the calendar and serves a large weather vane (whether). This symbolizes "then choose for yourselves this day whom you will serve, whether." The weather vane melts and re-solidifies into many golden idols (the gods). Your father serves each one the number "4" (forefathers served). Now imagine that a large swift river separates by some distance the butler from the idols (beyond the River). All these images mean "whether the gods your forefathers served beyond the river."

To cue the connecting word "or," visualize an oar lying across the river as a bridge. A man in a gleaming suit of armor (Amorites) strides over the oar carrying the idols (gods) under his arms. This scene signifies the phrase "or the gods of the Amorites." To picture the next phrase, "in whose land you are living," imagine the man in the suit of armor building a house from the sod of the land and stuffing a letter "U" down the chimney.

To start the final sentence, picture a cigarette butt (But) popping out of the chimney and landing in Joshua's trumpet. Joshua then walks up to the sod house and embraces or holds it (household); this means, "But as for me and my household." Together Joshua and the sod house approach and serve a throne. This completes the verse, "we will serve the Lord."

If you have vividly imagined these mental pictures, you will have stored Joshua 24:15 in your memory. Simply by recalling the first image, which represents the chapter and verse, the whole sequence of pictures should appear in your mind one at a time. As they do, by association you will be able to translate the pictures into a word-for-word recall of the scripture. Try it a few times, and reinforce any pictures or meanings that are unclear. After practicing this method for awhile, I believe that you will find it increasingly easy to memorize scriptures verbatim.

Grow Spiritually Through Memorizing

As you etch the Bible in your memory, you will grow spiritually. Even if the physical body is well fed, the spirit within may be starving. For we are more than flesh and bone; we are made in God's image (Gen. 1:26). Therefore, we have a soul, a spirit that needs to be nurtured. One who feeds only the body and starves the soul will never be fully content. As Christ so fitly spoke, "Man does not live on bread alone, but on every word that comes from the mouth of God" (Mt. 4:4).

It is my sincere prayer that you "like newborn babes, long for the pure milk of the word" (I Pet. 2:2 NASV) and that by memorizing portions of the Bible you will quench your thirst.

CHAPTER THIRTEEN

How to Apply Memory Skills as a Bible Teacher

Perhaps the most harrowing question that a Bible teacher can ask is simply, "What did we study last week?" The question is nerve-wracking because it reveals the amount of material that the class has truly learned, for true learning occurs only when the students can reproduce in their own minds the Bible knowledge that has been taught. If the class mutters just a few generalities about the prior lesson, and struggles to recall its content in any detail, the value of the Bible study is greatly diminished.

The whole point of teaching is to implant knowledge in the student's mind and to change his or her thoughts and actions. Probably every Bible teacher has been disheartened at one time or another by the lack of long-term learning in the classroom; nevertheless, this situation is easily remedied. Bible teachers that understand how to apply memory skills can increase not only their own recall of Bible study but their students's recall as well.

Assisting your class to remember Bible lessons involves all of the memory techniques and principles presented in Part II. You will increase your students's recall when you: 1) engage their interest and involvement, 2) provide structure in your lessons and explain patterns in the material, 3) optimize review through the proper timing and repetition of the material, and 4) form associations and create visual memory aids. All of the techniques that increase your recall will increase your students's recall, too.

Involve the Student

Perhaps the most effective method of improving student recall is simply to involve them personally in the class. A Chinese proverb reads: "Tell me, I'll forget. Show me, I may remember. But involve me and I'll understand." Understanding and retention grow as the student becomes more directly involved in the class and the material being taught. To accomplish this, impact as many of the senses as possible.

Realizing the power of visualization, a teacher should employ the sense of sight as often as possible. Use as many types of visual aids as practical. Besides using prepared visual aids, such as films, filmstrips, posters, and maps, merely writing key points on a chalkboard will greatly improve a student's recall. A simple written handout containing an outline of the lesson also works well. Encourage notetaking, for this reinforces the material through the sense of sight as well as the kinesthetic sense. Because reading involves sight, include scripture recitation in your class, too. Of all the avenues of learning and recall that we humans possess, sight is the most important; so create Bible lessons with visual impact.

Of course, you hope that your students are using their sense of hearing, otherwise little is going to be learned; however, the student will particularly remember the sound of his or her own voice. Hence, encourage discussion among the students when possible. Not only will this improve listening, it will most likely promote interest, too. A lively discussion is much more likely to be remembered than a dry lecture.

If you teach young children, you already know that they need an active and stimulating environment in which to learn. To help them recall your lesson and to even memorize scriptures, you may wish to employ action and body movement.

Let me give you one example of how to use body movement to help very young children memorize John 3:16a. Instead of orally repeating the verse many times, which involves only hearing, why not encourage the children to act out the verse. This will involve their whole body. You might try doing it this way: "For God" (point to the sky), "so loved" (hands on your heart), "the world" (join hands overhead in a big circle), "that he (point to the sky again), "gave" (arms extended in giving), "his one" (hold up one finger), "and only Son" (cradle your arms as if holding a baby). Repeat these actions a few times while saying the verse, and the children will learn and remember it more easily.

As you learned in chapter 6, interest and emotion stimulate good recall; therefore, do not neglect the value of a positive and buoyant atmosphere in your Bible class. If the excitement and the joy of learning God's Word radiates from the teacher, it will surely be felt by the students. Consider imitating David as he, with great emotion, sang the praises of God's Word:

> Because I love your commands more than gold, more than pure gold, and because I consider all your precepts right, I hate every wrong path. Your statues are wonderful; therefore I obey them. The entrance of your words gives light; it gives understanding to the simple. I open my mouth and pant, longing for your commands. (Ps. 119:127-131).

Provide Structure

Besides involving the sense of sight, providing the class with a written outline of the lesson also enhances memory by revealing the structure of the material. If you give the students a road map of the lesson, they will follow you more closely and thus recall more of the lesson. The outline allows the class to anticipate where you are going and why. This increases their understanding and recall. If you are unable to write an outline, even a verbal statement about the direction and purpose of the lesson will favorably orient the class.

Where possible identify the patterns or structure in the Bible text that you are teaching. For example, Christ employs structure and logic quite effectively in His great Sermon on the Mount.

Notice in Matthew 6:25-34 how Christ begins with concrete concepts and shifts gradually to abstracts concepts. First, He observes the workings of the natural world,

God's care of plants and animals. Then He compares the importance of plants and animals to the importance of mankind. From this comparison, He logically concludes that if God will care for the plants and animals, He will care for man. Finally, He recommends that since God will care for us, we should "seek first his kingdom and his righteousness" (Matt. 6:33). Christ begins with a kingdom that we can see, namely the plant and animal kingdom, and through a logical development He teaches about an unseen kingdom, the kingdom of heaven. Revealing structures and logical patterns such as these will help your students retain and recall your Bible lessons.

Use Concrete Terms

It has been said that for effective teaching, "The truth must be set in pictures that can be readily understood and applied." This is certainly true and is quite evident in the teachings of Christ. Let's examine Matthew 6:25-34 again to observe how Christ employs this technique to impart the content of His lesson in a memorable way. For example in verse 26, He directs attention to birds by saying, "Look at the birds of the air, that they do not sow, neither do they reap." He continues by pointing to the lilies and grasses of the field. As we already noted, Christ first introduces concrete items before He shifts to abstract concepts. This aids recall and understanding because the mind grasps and relates to concrete subjects much more readily than to abstract ones. Jesus often translated abstract ideas into concrete ones in order to make the Word of God understandable and memorable to all men.

A further example of this technique is Christ's teaching in parables, His earthly stories with a heavenly meaning. Jesus compared the kingdom of heaven to a mustard seed (Mark 4:30-32), to a growing seed (Mark 4:26-29), to yeast (Luke 13:20-21), to a merchant looking for fine pearls (Matt. 13:45), and a treasure hidden in a field (Matt. 13:44). Thus He illustrated the attributes of the kingdom of heaven in tangible terms that would be easy to grasp.

Therefore, using Christ's example, tell your lessons in concrete, tangible terms that will impress the senses. Let these terms introduce the teaching of more general, abstract concepts.

Always Review

Christ is truly the Master Teacher, and following his example will make you a better teacher. In the verses that we just examined in Matthew 6, He uses another memory enhancing technique, review. Public speakers are encouraged to tell their audiences three things: 1) Tell them what your are going to tell them (structure), 2) Tell them (content), and 3) Tell them what you told them (review). Christ does just that! In verse 25, He begins by telling the people what He will tell them, "do not be anxious for your life." Then He tells them why, using the logical argument that we discussed earlier (v.26-30). Finally, He reviews by telling them what He just told them, "Do not be anxious, then" (v.31).

Christ obviously understood the value of review. Because it is vital to long-term memory, each Bible lesson should include at least two periods of review, one at the beginning and one at the end. The start of a class is a good time to review the prior week's lesson. Because I employ visual memory aids, we review them together in our mind's eye and discuss how they relate to last week's lesson. After establishing that everyone can recall the mental pictures, which fixes the factual content of the lesson in the memory, we review the material in another important way, through restatement.

Using the recall of memory aids as a cue, I encourage the class to discuss the meaning and application of the lesson in their own words. This is a critical step in the learning and remembering process, for as we previously noted, true learning occurs only when the students can reproduce for themselves the Bible truths that have been taught.

A review near the end of the class period is also beneficial because most forgetting occurs in the first few minutes and hours immediately after learning. In fact, as much as 50% can be forgotten in just the first hour following learning. Acknowledging this fact, a review near the end of your Bible class will definitely help your students remember the lesson later. During this period of review, re-examine the highlights of the lesson that you have just taught. If possible, urge the students to review by restating the significant points. Coming at a critical time in the forgetting process, this period of reevaluation will firmly secure the lesson in the memory of your students.

In addition to regular reviews during each lesson, I heartily recommend entire class periods devoted to review. In my experience these classes are generally very satisfying and enjoyable to both student and teacher, particularly if all have been working hard on memory. At least one review class per 13-week quarter is helpful. If possible, end a particular series of Bible lessons with a review class. If you are using visual memory aids, the students will probably be able to recall the material quite fluently. After reviewing the details of the material, explore its meaning relative to daily Christian living.

This should produce a lively and fruitful discussion. And so it should, for gains in Bible knowledge are pointless unless they become a "working knowledge." As the apostle John wrote, "let us not love with words or tongue but with actions and in truth" (1 John 3:18). The ultimate review is usage, knowledge in action. As a Bible teacher encourage your students to apply their understanding of the Scriptures in their daily Christian lives.

Employ Association

When applying memory aids in teaching, the power of associations should never be overlooked. The mind absorbs and stores new information by association. Any steps that increase the strength and number of associations will increase the student's learning and recall.

As you study a particular Biblical topic, show its relation to other portions of the Bible and to prior studies made by the class. The greater the number of cross references or connections that you make between what you are currently studying and what the students already know, the greater will be their recall of your lesson.

With practice you can create your own visual memory aids for your class. Using the examples in this book as a guide, devise your own visual memory schemes to help your class remember the material that you are teaching. If you learn to employ these techniques in your private Bible study, inventing some visualization for classroom use will not be difficult.

From personal experience I can testify that most students enjoy the visualization exercises and are pleasantly surprised by the positive results. They are more fun than they are work; and yet, they are so effective in increasing recall.

I'm sure that after going through a few of the memory schemes you will feel the urge to build some yourself. I believe that you'll find it both fun and fruitful to learn God's Word this way, and I pray that you will feel as Jeremiah did when he said: "Thy words became for me a joy and the delight of my heart" (Jer. 15:16).

References Cited

Begley and others. 1986. "Memory," *Newsweek*, September 29, 1986: 48-54.

Burley-Allen. 1982. *Listening: The forgotten skill.* New York: John Wiley & Sons, Inc.

Furst, B. 1972. *Stop forgetting.* New York: Doubleday & Company.

Gallant, R. 1980. *Memory: How it works and how to improve it.* New York: Four Winds Press.

Haber, R. N. 1970. "How we remember what we see." *Scientific American*, 222(5): 104-112.

Loftus, E. 1980. *Memory: Surprising new insights into how we remember and why we forget.* Reading: Addison-Wesley Publishing Company.

Lorayne, H. 1975. Remembering people: *The key to success.* New York: Stein and Day.

Maltz, M. 1960. *Psycho-cybernetics.* New York: Pocket Books.

McKean, K. 1983. "Memory." *Discover*, 4(11): 19-28.

Psychology today: An Introduction 2d ed. Del Mar: CRM Books.